P9-BHT-181

HARD DRIVE

I appreciate the Todd family sharing this important story with the American people about how certain foreign actors, especially Chinese companies like Huawei, should be viewed with suspicion and concern. It's important for Congress to ensure that the federal government does all it can to protect national security and the safety of Americans, both at home and abroad, when challenged by foreign influences, especially countries like China that steal our technology and don't share our values. We should all keep Dr. Shane Todd's story and the Todd family's experience in mind as we consider future cooperation with certain countries and companies.

— **Congressman Frank R. Wolf**

A son murdered; a state that stonewalls an investigation; the U.S. government tacitly approving such stonewalling; a Chinese company that engages in economic espionage for military technology. The story, told by a determined mother who doggedly pursues the truth of her son's death, has elements of a detective novel and international intrigue, yet remains grounded in reason and facts. Hard Drive is an important work that should concern every American.

— **Mark T. Clark**, Ph.D.
Director, National Security Studies, California State University, San Bernardino
Member, Academic Advisory Board, NATO Defense College NRCC

Hard Drive is a heart-wrenching and inspiring story of a family's fight for truth in the murder of Dr. Shane Truman Todd, a young man of character who stood for his convictions against larger forces of power and evil. This story also contains important ramifications for national security. The wars of the future for American security will be fought not just on battlefields, but also on computers and in a business and technological context. This book is a must-read for anyone who cares about our country, justice, and national defense.

— **Glenn Gunderson**
Lead Pastor of Pomona First Baptist Church
Author of *Biblical Antidotes to Life's Toxins*

HARD DRIVE

*A Family's Fight
Against Three Countries*

MARY TODD AND
CHRISTINA VILLEGAS

NEW YORK

HARD DRIVE
A Family's Fight Against Three Countries

© 2015 **MARY TODD** AND **CHRISTINA VILLEGAS**.

All rights reserved. No portion of this book may be reproduced, stored in a retrieval system, or transmitted in any form or by any means—electronic, mechanical, photocopy, recording, scanning, or other,—except for brief quotations in critical reviews or articles, without the prior written permission of the publisher.

Published in New York, New York, by Morgan James Publishing. Morgan James and The Entrepreneurial Publisher are trademarks of Morgan James, LLC. www.MorganJamesPublishing.com

The Morgan James Speakers Group can bring authors to your live event. For more information or to book an event visit The Morgan James Speakers Group at www.TheMorganJamesSpeakersGroup.com.

A FREE eBook edition is available
with the purchase of this print book

CLEARLY PRINT YOUR NAME IN THE BOX ABOVE

Instructions to claim your free eBook edition:
1. Download the BitLit app for Android or iOS
2. Write your name in UPPER CASE in the box
3. Use the BitLit app to submit a photo
4. Download your eBook to any device

ISBN 978-1-63047-336-5 paperback
ISBN 978-1-63047-337-2 eBook
ISBN 978-1-63047-338-9 hardcover
Library of Congress Control Number:
2014943621

Cover Concept:
Jordan Doolittle

Cover Design by:
Rachel Lopez
www.r2cdesign.com

Interior Design by:
Bonnie Bushman
bonnie@caboodlegraphics.com

In an effort to support local communities, raise awareness and funds, Morgan James Publishing donates a percentage of all book sales for the life of each book to Habitat for Humanity Peninsula and Greater Williamsburg.

Get involved today, visit
www.MorganJamesBuilds.com

Habitat
for Humanity®
Peninsula and
Greater Williamsburg
Building Partner

To Our Country

TABLE OF CONTENTS

INTRODUCTION

When my Aunt Mary asked me to co-write a book about our family's fight to expose the truth concerning the death of my cousin, Dr. Shane Truman Todd, in Singapore, I was truly honored. My cousin Shane was one of my closest friends and a man of character.

From the time we were young, we could talk about anything, from life and love to religion and politics. In fact, Shane was rather like a brother to me because we are cousins on both my maternal and fraternal side. Shane's parents, Mary and Rick Todd, are my parents' siblings—my father is Mary's brother, and my mother is Rick's sister. Knowing Shane as well as I did genuinely benefited my life, and I hope that his story will benefit others by bringing more light to the universal struggle for truth and justice and the sinister nature of the powers seeking to suppress them. It should also concern those who take seriously U.S. national security. Shane's experience suggests that there are powerful actors around the world who may be seeking technologies that could threaten our country's interests—and they are willing to go to great lengths to advance that goal.

My family has always been proud of Shane and his accomplishments, yet not all of us shared his enthusiasm for taking a job overseas. But Shane wanted adventure and to experience the world. Thus, after completing his PhD in Electrical Engineering at the University of California, Santa Barbara in 2010, Shane accepted a job working for the Institute of Micro Electronics

(IME) in Singapore. He was intelligent, talented, and motivated, and his future looked bright.

About a year after moving to Singapore, however, Shane became uncomfortable with the society in which he was living. When he returned to the United States for a visit in December 2011, Shane and I discussed life in Singapore. Although Shane said he was enjoying his experience, he also said he felt uneasy living in a country where individuals are subordinate to an authoritarian state, under which people have no rights, but only duties. He noted that while Singapore is prosperous, orderly, and clean, it is, at the same time, dark and oppressive. It is a state in which political repression is legitimized through the delivery of economic prosperity, infrastructure, and the appearance of social order.

I believe that, at that time, my cousin already sensed the danger living in such a society would pose for anyone who might threaten the reputation or power of the state, himself included.

Shortly after this visit, Shane began to express explicit regret over moving to Singapore and fear that the work he was doing with a Chinese company could threaten his own security, as well as the interests of his country. Shane eventually resigned and found a new job in the United States—but he never made it home. Less than a week before Shane's scheduled return to the U.S., his girlfriend found him hanging in his apartment.

In spite of suspicious circumstances surrounding my cousin's death, no serious investigation took place. Officials called it a suicide, and that was supposed to be that. As our story reveals, the Singapore Police Force (SPF) and those involved in responding to and investigating Shane's death were grossly inept, if not actively complicit in covering up evidence that there was more to Shane's story. They have since sought only to prove the narrative of suicide, while concealing, destroying, or discrediting evidence indicating homicide.

Unfortunately, in Singapore, this behavior is not uncommon. According to the testimony of the SPF's supervising detective, out of over 100 suicides he had investigated, none turned out to be a homicide. Thus, the message is loud and clear: If you want to get away with murder in Singapore, make it appear to be a suicide.

Americans may not be surprised to learn this about Singapore. That's why perhaps the most disturbing part of our story is the role the U.S. government, specifically the State Department, has played in supporting the Singaporean rush to label this a suicide. The U.S. Embassy immediately declared that the inquiry into Dr. Todd's death was "comprehensive, fair, and transparent," and they have been unwilling to explain strong incongruities in their own actions and testimony. By legitimizing a grossly mishandled investigation and by showing a callous disregard for the death of an extremely accomplished American, our government is demonstrating a willingness to put diplomatic considerations above the protection and rights of its own citizens. In doing so, they are adopting the worst aspects of authoritarianism, which infect the executive and judicial processes in Singapore. When the U.S. government so flippantly dismisses the value of individual life, human rights, and judicial integrity abroad, Americans' rights also become less secure at home.

From the beginning, my family has sought the truth, and this quest, while arduous and full of seemingly insurmountable obstacles, has not changed. In telling the story of a family's fight for truth and justice from the perspective of Mary Todd, a mother who lost her first-born son, we seek to encourage those who have experienced tragedy, to warn fellow Americans of the dangers our country is facing, and to inspire and embolden those fighting their own battles against those who insidiously seek to gain and maintain power. We also hope that, at the conclusion of the book, the reader will share our conviction that Shane Todd died an American hero.

—**Christina Villegas**

Chapter 1

THE SMALL DARK ROOM

The Singapore Police Station, June 27, 2012. Investigating officer (IO) Khal ushered us into a scanty, putrid green room with no windows or pictures hanging on the wall. It felt like an interrogation room for criminals, not a room to console anguished, grieving parents. IO Khal took the chair behind the desk, offering Rick and me the two chairs facing it. There was barely enough room for the fourth chair that was brought from another room for Traci Goins, Vice Consul to the American Embassy. Rajina, the assistant in training, was crammed in the corner and forced to stand for the duration of the meeting, which lasted for several hours. The room was so cramped that when anyone needed to leave, everyone had to stand up and rearrange the chairs to create enough space to open the door.

Khal was a twenty-three year old police rookie, with a constant wide, sloppy grin, making it appear as if he were about to blurt out the punchline to a joke, rather than convey the worst news any parent could ever hear. He started off the meeting bluntly by asking, "Do you want to know how your son killed himself?"

We numbly nodded our heads. Khal began methodically reading from a typed sheet of paper a well-written, detailed description of how they concluded our first-born son Shane Truman Todd took his own life.

The description read more like a novel than a report written by the police: "First he fashioned an elaborate hanging apparatus that included drilled holes into the bathroom wall, bolts, pulleys, and ropes wrapped around the toilet and slung over the bathroom door. On the outside of the closed bathroom door he put the noose around his neck, stood on a chair and dropped to his death."

As I listened to the graphic depiction of how my son allegedly killed himself, I was dismayed: "It would take an engineer to design and build something so intricate...someone brilliant like Shane. Is it possible that my son could have taken his own life?"

It felt like an out-of-body experience as I contemplated the incredible possibility that I could have missed the signs: "How could my son, a man who loved life, family, and God and who had never been a quitter, so thoughtlessly take his own life without warning?" I was lost in turmoil, struggling between the conviction that I did know my son and anguished wondering if I really didn't know him at all. Yet, I had to believe the facts that were so meticulously laid out before us.

After reading the description of suicide, Detective Khal informed us that Shane had written two suicide notes: "I found the suicide notes in Shane's apartment on his open computer that was sitting on top of his bed. No one has read them before now. I printed up a copy for each of us. Would you like to read them, and is it all right if I give Ms. Goins and myself a copy?" With our approval, he ceremoniously handed out the notes.

As my brain absorbed the words I was reading, I felt my first sense of joy since learning of my son's death. The style of writing was completely foreign to me. The notes—addressed "Dear Everyone," "Dear Mom and Dad," "Dear John, Chet, and Dylan," "Dear Shirley," and "Dear Friends"—were written methodically, without emotion, as if the author were following a checklist of points that needed to be covered. They were void of the tortured despair that a man would express before ending his life. The notes did not contain one memory that held an important spot in our family's history. There were only two cold sentences to his three brothers, John, Chet, and Dylan, whom he loved beyond measure. The vernacular was not my son's and one of the memories, "drinking Shirley temples on the beach," never happened. I knew, right then and there, that if my son did not write the suicide notes, he did not commit suicide. It wasn't until almost a year later that my initial conviction about the notes was scientifically substantiated.

With a forceful look, I captured Khal's eyes and calmly handed the notes back to him: "My son might have committed suicide, but he did not write these notes."

Two days later, Rick and I, along with two of our sons, John and Dylan, anxiously headed to the apartment where Shane had lived and died. As I climbed the long, narrow staircase to Shane's apartment, my whole body was shaking, and my heart was pounding. My thoughts kept returning to the detailed description of how Shane supposedly hanged himself, so I was unnerved when we opened Shane's apartment door and realized it was unlocked and there was no crime-scene tape or signs of dusting for fingerprints.

Because something so horrendous had taken place in that apartment, I expected to be overcome with a sense of evil. I felt nothing. There was no sense of darkness, and the apartment did not look like a place where life was eliminated. It simply looked like someone was packing to leave—boxes of books, bags packed, clothes being washed, and price tags on furniture. The scene looked so normal that I expected Shane to walk out of the back room and greet us with his glowing smile and one of his famous bear hugs.

With the sheer determination of a mother on a mission, I made a beeline for Shane's bathroom. As I looked into the bathroom, I was perplexed and shocked. Nothing I saw matched IO Khal's description. "Oh my gosh, John, come quickly, you've got to see this," I yelled.

John ran to me and we both began to exclaim, "Where are the bolts, the ropes, and the pulleys? Why is the toilet not across from the door as Khal described it?" Perplexed, we ran our hands over the marble walls searching for holes that might have been patched, looking for anything that would back up what Khal had told us. Nothing!

The disparity between what I found in the bathroom and what IO Khal had told us confused me. As an ordinary, middle-aged, middle-class American, I had been brought up to believe that the job of the police is to protect citizens and to conduct thorough investigations to uncover what is true. I began to realize I had been naïve for thinking the SPF shared our concern for the truth, much less for our son.

I called Khal immediately and asked him to come to Shane's apartment to explain the obvious discrepancies between what he had read to us and the physical evidence. Khal and another tall man, with a turban wrapped around his head, arrived shortly. "Khal," I asked, "where are the bolts, the pulleys, the ropes, and why is the toilet in the wrong place?" Khal nervously responded that I must have misunderstood. I knew that I had not misunderstood a thing. Every word of that description was seared into my memory.

I called Traci Goins and asked her to tell me what she remembered from the description Detective Khal had read to us. She recounted the bolts, the ropes, the pulleys, slung over the toilet behind the door, and then over the bathroom door. I informed Traci that none of the physical evidence lined up with the written explanation that Rick had heard, that she had heard, and that I had heard from Detective Khal.

Khal and the man with him looked upset and kept trying to recreate different scenarios of how Shane could have hanged himself. As they were conjecturing, John tested each of the scenarios, and nothing they came up with would have been physically possible.

Thinking that actual evidence from the scene of death might clear up the confusion, I asked Khal if the police had taken pictures of Shane hanging from the door. Khal replied that the police had not taken pictures of him hanging because they were more worried about saving his life. This did not make sense: The police had previously told us that Shane had been dead for at least one to two days when he was found.

Khal said that pictures were taken of Shane's body lying on the bedroom floor, but when I asked him for these pictures and a copy of the description that he had read to us the day before, he said he could not give them to me because the case was still under investigation. Khal left Shane's apartment with a promise to get back to me with answers to all of my questions within the next day or two. He never did.

We lingered in Shane's apartment from morning into the late evening trying to find any clues about what had happened to our son. We kept prodding one another to continue searching: "Surely Shane would have left a clue."

As we packed up some of Shane's things to take home, I came across what appeared to be a little speaker for a MAC computer. "Do you think one of the boys could use this?" I asked Rick.

"Throw it in the bag," he responded.

It wasn't until weeks after Shane's funeral that Rick plugged in that "MAC speaker" and discovered that it was not a speaker at all, but an external hard drive with thousands of files backed up from Shane's computer. The data revealed by those files began to transform this story from a tragic suicide to an international saga of mystery, deceit, and cover-up involving three countries.

Chapter 2

BEFORE DEATH

We celebrated our last Christmas together as a complete family at the Todd family lake house in Marion, Montana. In the days leading up to Christmas, my heart was overflowing with joy. Shane was on his way home from Singapore to spend a two week vacation with the family before he headed to New Jersey for special training. I could not wait to have all four of my sons together again for the first time in nearly a year.

Even filling Shane's Christmas gift list brought me joy and laughter. The list was so Shane: amusingly practical and detailed. At the top of his list was a huge golf bag. When I asked Shane, who was not a golfer, why he wanted a golf bag he explained that the international airport fees on luggage do not apply to golf bags, so he could travel cheaper by putting his clothes and personal articles in one. He also asked for toiletries, because they were less expensive in the U.S. than in Singapore, and finally for a life vest and wetsuit for his latest hobby, kitesurfing.

Sadly, Shane's trip home was not the completely relaxing vacation he had hoped for. For the first time, he seemed unhappy and stressed about the work he was doing in Singapore. He was anxious and perturbed that his company, IME, had sent him on vacation with a tremendous workload. Although Shane felt that he was treated better than most, he did not like the way his colleagues were often mistreated. He complained that IME had a corrupt culture and that its employees were overworked and underappreciated. Shane also told us of his dissatisfaction with Singapore generally saying, "Singapore looks good on the outside, but it's oppressive on the inside. It is not a place where I want to live or raise a family." He made it clear that he was only going to work at IME for the three years he had already committed to.

Shane seemed additionally anxious about the impending training he was to receive in New Jersey. One afternoon, midway through his visit, Shane and his youngest brother Dylan were talking on the deck of the lake house overlooking the picturesque mountain range surrounding Bitterroot Lake. Shane told Dylan that he was worried about the training he would be doing on a multimillion-dollar MOCVD (Metal Organic Chemical Vapor Deposition) machine that IME had purchased from a New York company called Veeco. With concern in his eyes, Shane explained that this was a highly technical machine with the ability to rapidly advance telecommunication. When Dylan curiously asked Shane for more details about the machine and the training, Shane confided, "There is something weird that they're asking me to do. They told me that they're going to leave me alone in a room with the computer screen open with recipes for the MOCVD machine. I am supposed to hand write these recipes down. For some reason they can't give me the recipes directly."

Dylan, struck by the fact that this didn't seem right, responded, "That seems pretty shady, dude."

Shane replied, "Yeah, it does seem shady, but that's what I've been told to do, and I guess that's the way they do it."

It wasn't until months later, that Dylan realized the importance of that conversation on the deck at the lake that day.

In spite of Shane's workload, our last two weeks with him were rich, filled with ski trips and hikes, lots of eating, music, time on the lake, gut-splitting laughter, and generally reflecting and catching up on each other's lives. We enjoyed every minute of having Shane home.

After a delightful time together, my heart was heavy as I stood at the airport and said good-bye to my son. I sent Shane off with hugs, kisses, and tears, not knowing when he would be able to visit again. He turned around and waved goodbye one last time as he headed to catch his flight, and with a smile on his face, he assured me that he would call as soon as he got to New Jersey. I had no idea that this would be the last time I would ever lay my eyes on one of the greatest loves of my life. Even now, just writing the words on this page brings home the incredible, almost unimaginable fact that I will never see my son again in this life. It is a shocking reality that I am forced to face every single day for the rest of my life.

Shane called several times from New Jersey, reporting that the Veeco training was going well and that it was far more organized and informative than he had anticipated. He seemed relieved as he enthusiastically told me how excited he was to implement everything he was learning.

This enthusiasm began to fade, however, after Shane returned to Singapore in January. Following his return, we spoke via Skype every week for an hour or more. During one of those calls, Shane told Rick and me that he was extremely upset that the room IME had set aside for the MOCVD machine had been changed to a smaller room. He told us that the smaller room would not work for the machine, saying, "It's impossible, it won't work, something weird is going on. I don't understand what my boss Patrick Lo is doing."

Over subsequent calls, Shane seemed increasingly agitated with what was going on at IME. He specifically expressed concern over meetings with a Chinese company, saying "I am the only Anglo, in a group of Chinese people, who speak solely in Mandarin right in front of me. I have no idea what they're saying, but it makes me feel very uncomfortable." Shane told us that he felt so wary about his interactions with this Chinese company that he had bought language CDs in hopes of learning to understand Mandarin.

Shane's agitation eventually turned into fear as he told us he felt like he was being pressured to compromise U.S. interests. At one point he told me, "Mom,

I am in a terrible position, and if I go along with what they're asking me to do, I could be putting the security of our country in jeopardy, and I am not going to do it."

At first, I did not understand the gravity of what Shane was saying, and I thought he might have been being a little melodramatic. In fact, it wasn't until after Shane's death that I fully realized the important and sensitive nature of the technology Shane was using. I did start to take his concerns more seriously, however, when I received the following email from Shane, on February 25, 2012, asking Rick's and my opinion of an email he was formulating to send to his former PhD advisor, John Bowers:

Hi Mom and Dad,

I have been thinking about writing John Bowers to ask for his advice. Can you check out the draft below and tell me what you think? I want to be careful about this.

Love,
Shane

....

Hi John,

I appreciate your note about working together; it is something I would like to do. Unfortunately, I can't fully recommend working with IME. I have seen many questionable management practices and decisions in the last year and IME has become a difficult place to work. There are a lot of details to the story that I won't go into here, but one example that you know a bit about is the collaboration I tried to get going with Aurrion. When Alex and I tried to get a collaboration going between Aurrion and IME, we put a lot of effort into generating a plan for creating silicon interposers with integrated optics including the highbred laser made by Aurrion. After IME upper management reviewed the plan, they decided to forget the collaboration with Aurrion and try to build the hybrid lasers themselves. I almost feel as though they let me engage with Alex as much as possible so that they could collect information on how to build the laser. This is something that has bothered me immensely and has made me resistant to trying to engage any of my former colleagues into collaboration with IME.

As I have observed this and some other questionable practices and decisions, I have struggled with what I should do myself. On one hand, I feel it may be best for me to try to stay here until I find success in the project I am working on. On the other hand, I do not want to be part of an organization that operates in a way that is ethically questionable and stifling to the creative output of its employees. For the most part I've tried to maintain a good attitude, persevere, and continue to work hard. But now I am coming to the point where I think I may be better off in the long run if I come back to the states and start fresh at a new job. I know it is difficult to assess the situation as an outsider looking in, but if you have any advice that you feel may be helpful to me I would really appreciate it.

Thanks,
Shane

Sadly, Shane never sent that email to John Bowers, explaining to me by email:

Hi Mom,
    I think the content is okay but it might be a bit heavy for email. I was thinking maybe I could write something simple at first like:

Hi John,
    I would like to work with you in the future. Do you have something in mind? I have to admit I'm hesitant about setting something up through IME. Please let me know if you want to discuss some time.

Thanks,
Shane

In the end, right before he quit his job, Shane sent the simple email to John Bowers. After Shane's death, Rick shared the first drafted copy with John Bowers, and he responded, "If I had received that email from Shane, I would have told him to leave Singapore immediately." How I wish Shane would have sent that original email.

Following several weeks of turmoil, consideration, and prayer, Shane reluctantly tendered his resignation to IME, and turned in a 60-day notice. Shane's boss, Patrick Lo, was not happy, and begged him to stay. Lo told Shane he would do whatever it took to keep him at IME and told Shane that he would not receive his $22,000 bonus, unless he stayed until the end of June. Always the pragmatic one, Shane, not wanting to miss out on the bonus, agreed to stay until then.

Even after he agreed to this extension, Shane told me that the company was very unhappy with his decision to leave and, for the first time, he expressed concern for his life. He said, "Mom I might be paranoid, but I have the feeling that they are threatening my life if I don't stay." On several occasions, Shane lamented, "I am so naïve. Coming to Singapore was the worst mistake of my life." And, "If God gets me out of Singapore alive, I will give him all the honor and glory." Almost every conversation we had, Shane told us that he was afraid he would never see us again.

While Rick begged Shane to come home immediately if he really felt his life was in danger, Shane told his dad that he was a professional, and that he had signed a contract agreeing to give a sixty day notice before leaving. He was worried it would look bad to other companies if he didn't keep his word. Shane had always taken to heart one of Rick's favorite sayings that "a man without his word is nothing."

There were times that Shane vacillated in his decision about whether to leave or stay at IME. During one of our conversations, Shane said, "Maybe I should just stay at IME and fulfill my three year commitment."

I exclaimed, "Why would you stay with a company that you hate, that you think is corrupt, and that you believe is asking you to compromise US security?

Shane replied, "You are right Mom, I was trying to take the easy way out, I can't stay here."

In my American mindset, I could not truly fathom the seriousness of what Shane was telling us, and I always reassured him, "Shane, you're going to be fine. You quit your job and you have a ticket to come home."

Shane would respond by saying, "Thanks, Mom. I hope you're right. That makes me feel better."

As the weeks progressed, Shane's concern that his life was being threatened did not diminish. At the beginning of April, Shane called me and said, "Mom, I am going to call you every week. If a week passes and you don't hear from me, email me right away. If I don't call you back, call the American Embassy." When Shane did not call me within the week, I emailed him right away, and he called back apologizing, "Sorry Mom, I got so busy, I forgot to call you, I'm fine."

Even though I never believed that Shane would actually be murdered, I did start to worry a bit more and asked our family, friends, and fellow church members to pray for Shane's safety. I told many people about his situation, but I had so much confidence in Shane. He was a high school wrestling champion and an avid rugby player, and he was never afraid of a good fight—especially when it was for someone or something he loved.

One summer, for example, Shane was at the local rodeo in Kalispell, Montana with his brother John and his cousins Christina and Roston, when some drunken Montana cowboys, who did not like Californians, came up looking for a fight. When Christina urged the boys to calm down and reached her arm out to stop the impending duel, one of the cowboys pushed her. That was all it took. Shane turned his head to the side, spit on the ground, wheeled back towards the guy and started punching. The poor sap's friends backed away, as he fell to the ground in the fetal position to protect himself from Shane's blows. As Shane walked away, he growled, "Don't ever touch my cousin again." There were many times like that in Shane's life when he faced challengers or had to deal with adversity, and he always came out the victor. I couldn't help but believe that the same would be true again.

In spite of my concern over my son's safety, one of the greatest joys of my life was when, in the months leading up to his death, Shane told me about his renewed faith in God. Rick and I had raised our boys to be men of integrity, to love God, and to go to church. As a child, Shane had always done his best to live up to our high standards. In high school, he was an exemplary student and he took his faith seriously, even acting as a leader in his youth group. Once he got to college, however, Shane's faith began to wane. During one of his visits home, I was shocked when he told me he wasn't sure if he still believed in God. His science classes were deeply affecting him, and he was having a hard time reconciling what he was raised to believe and what he was learning in school. I was deeply burdened for my son, and I will never forget the thrill of the day, when Shane told me that he and his girlfriend, Shirley, were attending church together in Singapore. In one of our longer conversations shortly before his death, Shane asked to pray with me and I sat stunned in silence with tears trickling down my face as my son prayed a beautiful prayer acknowledging his love for and dependence on Christ. Remembering that prayer has been one of my greatest sources of comfort since Shane's death.

Shane's last days before his scheduled return on July 1, 2012 were filled with busy activity. He was working hard to finish up all of his responsibilities at IME and was diligently looking for a job back in the U.S. After carefully considering his options, Shane told me he was accepting an offer from a company called Nuvotronics in South Carolina.

Shane's last day of work at IME was Friday, June 22. With tickets bought, bags packed, and going away parties to attend, Shane started to feel a sense of relief, believing he was actually going to make it home. He had so much to look forward to. At Shane's request, we had agreed to wait for his return to celebrate Father's Day and his brother Dylan's 21st birthday. He was also honored and excited that his cousin Katie had asked him to be in her wedding that summer, and he had arranged to stay at his grandmother Jean's apartment in California and borrow her car, while she was in Montana, before starting his new job. His future seemed bright.

It was only shortly after his death, upon receiving an e-mail from David Sherrer, the president of Nuvotronics, that we fully realized how bright Shane's future really was. The e-mail to Rick began: "Dear Mr. Todd, I cannot begin to say how sorry I am for you, and Shane's family and friends." Mr. Sherrer continued on to emphasize how impressed he was with Shane and his work, stating, "Of the dozens of candidates we interviewed, Shane stood out as our very top choice. This despite having little experience (compared to some candidates with 20 to 30 years' experience). We believed and were willing to bet that Shane would exceed them all. For us, there was no close second choice… I don't know where Shane's career would have taken him, but I am confident he would have helped to change an industry…"

Chapter 3

NEVER THE SAME

Dear Rick and Mary,

How does one address the unthinkable, the unfathomable, the impossible? All we poor humans have is paltry, inadequate words. They are so insufficient—but they are all I have to offer; words of sorrow and always words of love. As I went about the silly business of the day—the club, the grocery store, Target, et al.—my mind was on the everyday aspects of life, and how your everyday living will never ever be the same...

ait a minute—STOP! I am Mary Todd. I live a charmed life. I am the one who comforts and helps others, not the other way around. How could these beautifully penned words be intended for me?

The morning of June 24, 2012 was cool and crisp. The sun was already bright and the water was shimmering like diamonds across Bitterroot Lake. I woke up thinking it was going to be a great day. Rick was in route home from Narita, Japan. My second oldest son John and my youngest son Dylan were visiting for the weekend and staying with my other son Chet and his wife Corynne at our family-run bed and breakfast. My mom (Granna) was visiting from California, and was staying with me at the lake house. As my mom and I sat wrapped in our cozy bathrobes, enjoying each other's company over a hot cup of coffee, I couldn't help thinking, "Life can't get any better than this."

After we finished our coffee, I uncharacteristically decided to check my Facebook page. I was immediately surprised to see a private message from Shane's girlfriend Shirley, a Filipino nurse whom Shane had met on a dating site in Singapore. My heart froze as I read Shirley's urgent request for my contact information. I knew right away that something was wrong, but I never imagined how wrong. I sent Shirley my information and then sent Shane the last email I would ever write him, "Hi Shane, Please call me ASAP. LOVE YOU, Mom."

Waiting for the phone to ring seemed like an eternity. My mom, always the optimist, kept reassuring me, "Relax, I'm sure Shane is fine."

"Mom!" I replied, "Shirley has never contacted me before. I have never met her or even spoken to her by phone. I know that something is wrong! Either Shane is sick or he has been in a bad accident."

As my anxiety grew, I could hardly breathe. When I couldn't take it anymore, I called John, hoping he would be able to think of a way to get a hold of Shane. My call woke him up from a dead sleep. Alarmed by the early call, he sat straight up in bed and asked, "What's up, Mom?"

Trying to maintain control, I burst out, "John, I'm really worried about your brother. Shirley left me a message on Facebook, asking for my contact information. I've got to get in touch with Shane. Do you have a way of contacting him?"

In his husky morning voice, John tried to calm me down, "Don't worry, Mom. I'm sure it's nothing. No, I don't have any way to contact Shane. He always calls me, and I don't have his number. Call me when you hear from Shirley, and try not to get too upset."

Twenty excruciatingly long minutes later, around 7:30, the phone rang. My heart skipped a beat when I saw the out-of-country number on my caller ID. Thank God, it had to be Shirley, or Shane. "Hello, hello…" All I could hear on the other end of the line was shrill, ear-piercing screaming. "Shirley, is that you?" I pleaded, "Please calm down Shirley, I can't understand you."

Finally, through the crying and screaming, I began to decipher the words that would forever change my life, "Shane hanged himself! I found him hanging from his bathroom door!"

My brain could not absorb the reality of what Shirley was saying. I kept thinking, "This couldn't be true. Shirley must be mistaken." All at once, the impact of those tragic words hit me like a punch to the kidney, and I fell to my knees and cried out, "No, God, please, no. My son DEAD…Suicide…how could this be?"

After I picked myself up off the floor and regained some composure, I told Shirley how sorry I was that she had to witness such a horrendous thing. I tried to get more details, but it was fruitless. She was inconsolable. Our conversation ended with my promise that we would be on a plane to Singapore as soon as humanly possible.

Robotically, I called Rick to tell him something no parent should ever have to hear. I needed to hear his voice, but I didn't know how I was going to tell him. Rick's voicemail picked up immediately, which indicated that he was still in the air, so I left a message telling him to call me ASAP.

Next, I knew I had to call the boys to tell them that their oldest brother, best friend, protector, and mentor had taken his own life. This was the hardest call I have ever made. While I needed my boys more than ever and I longed to hold them in my arms, I dreaded seeing the torment and horror that would be on their faces.

My mom held me as we waited for the boys to drive the eight miles from the B&B to the lake house. Corynne, with God's strength and grace, stayed behind to continue serving the B&B guests. Tidal waves of pain would hit me and I would fall to the ground, lying flat on my back, kicking my legs up and down, screaming a primal cry.

When the boys arrived, we all held each other and sobbed. At one point, Chet said, "Suicide is so selfish. I can't believe Shane did this to us. I am furious with him."

Dylan was quiet, while John occupied his time trying to figure out the quickest way to get to Singapore.

Within a half hour of the boys' arrival, Rick landed in Denver. After listening to my message, he knew something very bad had happened, so he called me before he even deplaned. The only way I could figure for breaking the worst news of our lives was to be simple and straight forward: "Honey, I have terrible news. Shane hanged himself. He is dead." Rick, sitting in the midst of strangers, let out a scream and dropped his cell phone.

After making plans to meet Rick at the Denver airport, John, Dylan, and I started packing. Chet and Corynne, because of the guests at the B&B, could not go with us. I was so grateful my mother was there to help them endure this unthinkable experience.

I cannot imagine how Rick survived the four, long hours alone at the Denver airport—confused, sleep deprived, and in pain, waiting for us to join him. When we arrived, I threw myself into his waiting arms. Without words, our eyes engaged, the pain was so raw and real: Our first-born son was dead!

As Rick and John, both airline pilots, sat together trying to figure out how to get to Singapore, my cell phone rang. It was my brother Richard. As we talked, I could tell Richard wanted to tell me something, but he seemed hesitant. Finally, he proceeded cautiously, "Mary, Shane had expressed fear and concern to you over his job. Something doesn't seem right. I'm not sure Shane killed himself."

This was the first time that I considered anything other than suicide. In my hazy state of overwhelming grief, the thought of murder had not crossed my mind. His comment made a light go on. I responded, "Richard, you're right. I can't believe I didn't think of that myself."

Richard then warned me, "We really have to be careful not to believe something just because we want it to be true, but I am doubtful that Shane would have committed suicide."

Richard told me that he had spoken to a computer forensic expert that morning, who had emphasized that if we got possession of Shane's computer, we should not turn it on or open any files. Doing so before the hard drive had been encased would ruin the evidentiary value of anything on Shane's computer. This turned out to be incredibly valuable advice.

I thanked Richard for his input and we hung up. The fog was beginning to lift, and I began to think more clearly. For the past four months, Shane had been telling me he was worried about his work and feared for his life. While I knew I needed to consider all evidence, even if it didn't support what I wanted to believe, I contemplated for the first time the real possibility that my son did not kill himself, but was a victim of murder.

When I told the boys what Uncle Richard had said, they both responded they had thought the same thing from the beginning, but were afraid to say anything. Rick said that idea had also entered his mind, but that he thought it best to wait until we saw the evidence before formulating any opinion.

From Denver we flew to California, where we spent the night before catching a flight to Singapore. We landed in Singapore on June 26, which was Dylan's 21st birthday. With broken hearts we faced the reality that we would not be celebrating this special day together in Montana as Shane had requested. Our lives would never again be the same.

Chapter 4

BLACK AND WHITE

Within 48 hours of hearing of Shane's death, we arrived in Singapore in the middle of the night with no place to stay. Thankfully, a dear friend had arranged to have two local pastors pick us up and help us find accommodations. After a couple hours of searching by phone for an available hotel, all six of us squeezed into a five-seat car with our luggage piled on our laps.

This was not my first trip to Singapore. When Shane was a baby, Rick, who was a navy pilot at the time, served two nine-month deployments on an aircraft carrier. Shane and I would often travel to a port to meet Rick's carrier and spend shore time there with him. One of those trips was to Singapore. We had a magnificent week, enjoying swimming, shopping, and an unforgettable dinner at the famous Raffles Hotel. At the time, I had been struck by how beautiful, clean, and safe Singapore appeared to be.

As we made the long, dark, hot ride from the airport to our hotel, the only thing I remember thinking was that Singapore was not the beautiful place I'd remembered. Beneath the seemingly perfect façade, the trees that lined the narrow streets looked like menacing tangled vines reaching out to grab and strangle me. The air was so humid that it was hard to breathe.

On the way to the hotel, we explained to the pastors what we had been told about Shane's death. We also shared our suspicions that Shane could have been murdered because of the fear he had expressed for his life. Both of them resolutely assured us that Singapore is one of the safest countries in the world— that "there is no murder in Singapore." I can't count how many times we heard that definitive mantra: "THERE IS NO MURDER IN SINGAPORE!"

By the time we got to the hotel, we only had a few hours to sleep before our scheduled 11:00am meeting at the Singapore Police Station. But I couldn't sleep, so I called Shirley to let her know we had arrived. She wasn't sleeping either, so she told me she'd grab a cab and be right over. Within twenty minutes, Shirley and I were in each other's arms, hugging and crying, both of us trying to make sense of what had happened to Shane. I was surprised by how comfortable I felt with Shirley, a total stranger. There was none of the awkwardness usually associated with meeting someone for the first time. I guess our mutual pain drew us together. Not wanting to wake the others, we sat out by the hotel swimming pool, and Shirley began to tell me the whole story from the beginning.

Instead of trying to recollect exactly what Shirley said, I have included direct wording from her conditional statement to the Singapore police. The only changes that have been made in it are grammatical.

I last saw Shane over the weekend, from 16 June 2012 (a Saturday) to 18 June 2012 (a Monday).

Shane and I had dinner on 16 June 2012 and I spent that night at his apartment.

On 17 June 2012 (a Sunday), after going to church together in the morning, we went cycling to Changi Beach Park. After spending the whole day together, I spent the night again at Shane's apartment.

We left Shane's apartment on 18 June 2012 at about 8am. Shane was going to work. I was returning to my own apartment. Shane told me that this was his last week at IME. He also told me that he had already bought a ticket for a flight back to America on

1 July 2012. He further said that he would be settling errands this week. These errands included selling office furniture. Shane also wanted to cancel his mobile phone and internet subscriptions. We bade each other goodbye that morning. It was the last time I saw Shane alive.

Shane and I did not usually talk to or text each other on weekdays because:

(a) I knew how busy Shane was at work; and

(b) Shane knew that I might be at work when he was at home.

Shane, however, never ignored any of my phone calls or texts.

Shane would usually contact me on Friday nights or Saturday mornings to inform me whether we would be meeting each other that weekend. After 18 June 2012 Shane did not text me. I did not contact Shane either.

On 20 June 2012 (a Wednesday) at about 8:37pm, I sent a text to Shane, telling him that I missed him. Shane replied about two hours later, telling me that he also missed me and that he was having dinner with his colleagues. That same night, at about 11 pm, Shane sent another text to me, telling me that he was going to sleep and that he would text me later. This was the last time I heard from Shane.

I did not hear from Shane on 22 June 2012 (a Friday). I waited until the morning of 23 June 2012 (a Saturday), but Shane still did not contact me. I did not send Shane a text because I thought that he was busy packing for his return to America or doing some other things.

On 24 June 2012 (a Sunday), as I was unable to take it and because it was unusual for Shane not to contact me, I sent a text to Shane at about 8:33am, asking him if he was all right. Shane did not reply. I then called Shane sometime between 1pm and 2pm, but he did not answer. I found it very unusual for Shane to ignore my text and call. I subsequently sent a text to Shane at about 6pm, asking him what was going on. I wanted to know if Shane was all right. In this text, I told Shane that if I did not hear from him, I would go to his apartment. I thought that Shane had fallen sick or was involved in an accident. I was very worried about him. Shane did not reply to my text.

As I was very worried about Shane and I was tired of waiting for him to reply, I took a taxi to his apartment. When I reached his apartment some time between 6pm and 7pm, I found the common main door to both of the units on the second floor unlocked. Shane occupied one of the units on the second floor while Michael William Goodwin ("Michael") occupied the other unit on the same floor. I entered Shane's apartment through its unlocked, but shut, door.

On entering Shane's apartment, I noticed that all of the lights in the apartment were off, except the lights in the master bedroom. The living room was quite messy, with clothes and boxes lying everywhere. Shane slept in the master bedroom. I could see the light in the master bedroom shining from under the door in the master bedroom. When I first saw this, I was upset, as I thought that Shane had been ignoring my calls and texts. I immediately walked towards the master bedroom and opened the door. On opening the door and looking to my left, I saw Shane's body leaning away from the door of the toilet in the master bedroom. Shane was in an upright position and he was leaning forward. I cannot remember if Shane's feet were on the floor. However, I remember that his face was all white but he was purple from his elbows down to his fingers and from his knees down to his toes. The purple color from Shane's elbow and from his knees was probably caused by blood pooling due to the effect of gravity. Every other part of Shane's body was white and there was hard fluid coming out of Shane's nose. I do not remember seeing any visible injuries on him. Shane's eyes were closed. I also recall seeing a black cord (the "black strap") hanging above Shane's head and around his neck. I am unable to describe how the blackstrap looked exactly, but I know it was thin. I do not remember if there was also a towel around Shane's neck. I do not remember if the air-conditioning in the room was on.

I also saw a wooden chair approximately 1.5 m from where Shane's body was hanging, near the wardrobe in the master bedroom. The wood chair was in front of Shane's hanging body.

The back of the wooden chair faced away from his body. I cannot remember if the wooden chair was on top of the towel. The wooden chair appeared to be one of the chairs from the dining set in the kitchenette of Shane's apartment. I cannot remember any other occasion where I had seen the wooden chair in the master bedroom. I've never seen a towel placed under any of the chairs of the dining room set in the kitchenette.

I remember seeing Shane's laptop on his bed. Shane's mobile phone was connected to the laptop. I cannot remember if I touched the laptop. I cannot remember if I touched anything in the master bedroom.

On seeing Shane's hanging body, I screamed in shock and ran out of the apartment and into the hallway, which led to the staircase landing. My screams alerted Michael, who was in his apartment on the same floor. Michael came out of his apartment unit and asked me what was going on. I cannot remember what I told Michael exactly, but I remember telling him to check Shane's apartment to confirm what I had seen. Michael did not enter Shane's apartment. Instead Michael proceeded to the ground floor of the property to call for the police. I then went back into the master bedroom and shook Shane's body back and forth from the front to ascertain whether he was dead or alive. I do not remember how many times I shook him, but I did it for about a few seconds. His body did not move when I shook it. He was also heavy. Shane did not respond or move and I left the master bedroom. As Shane's body did not swing when I shook it, I assume that his feet were on the floor; however, I did not see whether his feet were on the floor or if they were touching the floor. I only assume they were. The police came soon after.

I never had the keys to Shane's apartment. Shane would always lock the door to his apartment and the common main door when we left his apartment. However, whenever Shane invited me over to his apartment, he would leave the common main door and his apartment door unlocked.

Other information

I recall one occasion were Shane told me that there were "heavy hands" coming after him and that he was working on something that could get him into trouble with the American government. This concerned something about defense, but I did not understand what Shane was talking about. I thought Shane was joking. I told Shane that he was thinking too much and that he had nothing to worry about as he was going to leave Singapore in a few weeks. As Shane was a perfectionist, I thought that Shane was thinking too much and over analyzing. When I told Shane that he was thinking too much, he'd acknowledge that maybe he was. I did not speak to Shane about this matter again. I thought that Shane was going to be punished by his bosses for not performing his job well when he said that "heavy hands" were coming after him.

At 10:30am, Cordi, the human resources representative from IME, met us in the hotel lobby. Cordi was a large, striking woman, well dressed, with spiky heels. She was cheerful, but also appropriately displayed her condolences. She told us she was shocked by Shane's death—that everyone at IME was. She related what a great guy Shane was, and how much people liked him at work. When we asked her if he seemed depressed, she said no, that he was upbeat and friendly. She also mentioned that he was generous with his time and was always willing to help anyone in need.

Cordi let us know that IME would cover all of our hotel expenses, and they wanted to do anything they could to help make our time easier. Whatever we needed, however big or small, we were simply to let Cordi know, and she would do her best to accommodate. She also gave us two cell phones to use while we were in Singapore. We were surprised, and impressed with how generous and gracious IME was at that time.

Cordi also informed us that Shane had a hundred thousand dollar life insurance policy through IME, and that even though Shane had not named us as the beneficiaries, under the circumstances, we would be the recipients. She promised to make arrangements for us to see a lawyer, so we could retrieve the money as soon as possible. We were taken aback by this information because Shane had never mentioned a life insurance policy, and it seemed strange that Shane wouldn't have listed us as the beneficiaries. We later realized this life insurance policy wasn't just any life insurance policy, and that there was more behind this than it first appeared.

After arranging for a taxi to take us to the Singapore police station, Cordi sent us off with kind words, a hug, and a promise to keep in touch. Our drive to the police station felt like an episode of Dragnet. We were in a black and white taxi that reminded me of an old fashion police car. When I looked out the window everything appeared in black and white. The trees were in black and white. The cars were in black and white. The buildings were in black and white. The people, and even the foliage and the flowers, were in black and white. Over and over again, I thought to myself, "This is just a nightmare. Soon, I am going to wake up and find out that none of this is real."

Traci Goins, the vice consul to the American Embassy, met us at the police station. She was a hefty woman, with a kind face and soothing voice. She made me feel comfortable, and I liked her instantly. After we introduced ourselves, Rick asked Traci if we could speak to her privately before we met with the police. We left John and Dylan with the escorting officer, and took Traci off to a corner of the rundown police station.

Rick began by saying, "Traci, we need to know if we can trust the Singapore police?"

Traci looked puzzled, "Why, what are you worried about?"

Rick continued, "We're not sure whether to trust the police with the information Shane gave us before he died."

Traci intently questioned, "What did Shane tell you before his death that makes you suspicious?"

We told Traci about the Chinese company that made Shane feel uncomfortable. We told her about Shane's fear of compromising U.S. security. And we told her that, after he quit his job, Shane had related to us that he felt his life was being threatened.

Traci appeared to take our concerns seriously. She told us to wait while she called the embassy for advice. Traci was on the phone for 10-15 minutes with an unidentified person. We couldn't hear everything she was saying, but we could tell she was relaying what we had shared with her. After she hung up, she told us that the person she spoke with at the embassy felt that we could trust the Singapore police, and to go ahead and tell them everything we knew.

After signing in at the front desk and leaving our passports with the clerk, we were escorted through several doors to the main part of the station. A young man was waiting for us, who introduced himself as Investigating Officer Muhamad Khaldun Bin Sarif, but said we could call him "Khal." He also introduced us to his assistant in training, Rajina. Khal said he would first like to talk to Rick and me alone, and then he would interview the boys separately. We asked if Traci Goins could join us, and he said she could. The boys were taken to a separate waiting room, and Khal escorted us to the tiny interrogation room.

It was in that stuffy, oppressive room that Khal read the detailed description of how Shane supposedly hanged himself on his bathroom door. It was there that he handed us the alleged suicide notes. And it was there that he returned some of Shane's personal items, explaining that because the case was still under investigation, the SPF would retain Shane's computer, cell phone, and work diary. Rick took that statement as an opportunity to tell Khal what Shane had told us before his death. Grinning and indifferent, Detective Khal, told us that we could record any suspicions in our conditional statement.

For the next several hours, Rick and I worked on our conditional statements. Khal would ask questions, we would answer, and then he would type out our answers using his own words. He asked questions such as: "Is there a history of depression in your family? How long had Shane been depressed? Did you know about his relationship with Shirley? What kind of relationship did you have with Shane? Has he ever threatened to take his own life before? Did Shane have a good relationship with his brothers? Did Shane have friends? Described the kind of person Shane was. Why did Shane decide to leave IME? How would you describe Shane's mental condition at the time of his death?"

The questions went on and on, but none of them addressed our concerns about possible foul play. They were all related to finding out why Shane would commit suicide. Finally, Khal asked if I would like to add anything to the conditional statement. I resoundingly responded, "YES, I would like to say that my son did not write the suicide notes."

I then summarized a few of the blatant problems with the notes[1]: The notes are formal and cold with words and phrases Shane has never used. The language doesn't even sound like an American's. The notes begin with Shane thanking IME, but Shane had repeatedly told Rick and me that he hated IME. The notes also listed several vague memories starting with "drinking Shirley Temples on the beach." This memory never happened. We never drank Shirley Temples on the beach. And the other memories, while factual, are superficial and meaningless. We are a close-knit family full of significant and rich memories. If Shane had written these notes, he would have shared more profound and vital memories.

After giving my statement, I was exhausted and wanted to see John and Dylan. I excused myself from the dank interrogation room, and Rajina escorted me to the boys. The boys were relieved to see me and were full of questions. They listened dumbfounded, as I recounted the detailed description of how Shane supposedly hanged himself with bolts and pulleys. I then pulled out my copy of the alleged suicide notes and read them out loud.

Both boys were incensed, "those notes weren't written by Shane, they don't even sound remotely close to something Shane would write." We sat together somewhat bewildered, knowing that if Shane did not write those suicide notes, he did not commit suicide. A new question emerged: Just who had written the notes and what had really happened to Shane?

---

1   A more detailed description of the discrepancies in the alleged suicide notes will come later. The full content of the notes is included in Appendix A.

Chapter 5

STRENGTH TO FACE ANOTHER DAY

A t the end of our exhausting day at the police station, Traci offered to set up a meeting for the following day with the FBI at the American Embassy. She then graciously said, "You guys have had a rough day, why don't you join me for dinner? I will call my housekeeper and ask her to prepare one of her delicious home-cooked meals."

After a grueling day, I just wanted to get back to the hotel room and process everything we had seen and heard, and I was anxious to have our nightly Skype conversation with Chet and Corynne. I turned to Rick, and gave him a look that said, "I do not want to do this."

Rick whispered in my ear, "We can't say no to her kind offer." Unhappily, I knew he was right.

Upon arriving at Traci's flat, we were immediately set at ease by her fluffy, tail-wagging dog and her housekeeper, a delightful Hispanic woman, who greeted us with a glowing smile and warm hug. Traci's flat was elegant and comfortable, with a view overlooking the city. We sat in the spacious living room, sipping a glass of wine, looking at pictures, and hearing stories about Traci's life and her family. Focusing on something other than our horrendous situation was a welcome relief. After enjoying a tasty meal together, I thanked Traci for the peaceful evening and asked her how often she invited families she met through the embassy to her home. She replied that she'd only done it once before in her entire career. I will always be grateful for Traci's kindness and the reprieve she offered us that night.

Back at the hotel, I could not find the rest I so desperately needed. My night was long and excruciating. While Rick tried to sleep, I sat alone in the bathroom with a broken heart contemplating what we had to face in the morning when we were scheduled to identify Shane's body at the morgue.

I stayed up all night researching suicide by hanging on my computer. I discovered it is one of the most gruesome ways to die. I saw images of people with tortured, anguished looks of distress and faces stained with broken capillaries. The thought of my son in such a state was too much to bear. This was one of my darkest moments of despair. I was still awake at five in the morning when Rick joined me in the bathroom and began to pray for me. As he prayed, I felt an inexplicable and supernatural strength to face the day.

It was cloudy and dark when we arrived by taxi at the morgue. Not typical of Singapore, the conditions of the morgue resembled those of a third world country. It was disorganized, dirty, smelly, and there were people everywhere. The unfriendly clerk at the front desk told us that Shane's body was not ready yet and to take a seat. We waited in that hot, muggy morgue, with our legs sticking to the plastic chairs, for almost two hours. During that long wait, we witnessed the torment of families who had lost loved ones and mothers who were writhing in pain, screaming from the depths of their souls. It was so poignant that for a moment I forgot my own pain, and was filled with an overwhelming desire to minister to and pray for these poor, broken people. But then reality would hit like a tidal wave, and I would remember why we were there. We were in the same boat. We were one of these grieving families.

Strength to Face another Day | 31

Finally, a door swung open, and a loud voice called out the name Todd. The four of us stood up and, with trepidation, walked towards the door. We were escorted into a long hallway, with a big window covered by a rolled down shade. Slowly, the shade was lifted, and there, lying on a gurney, was Shane's body, covered by a sheet up to the top of his neck. A huge sense of relief washed over me as I saw my son's gorgeous face. There was no tortured look, no anguish, and no broken blood vessels. Shane looked peaceful and normal, as if sleeping. I could not take my eyes off of him. I was so happy to see him. Every fiber of my being yearned to touch him. If it weren't for the glass window separating us, I would have thrown my arms around him and kissed his face.

After what seemed like only a few minutes, the escort informed us that our time was up. I begged him, "Please give us more time."

He answered, "Sorry, there are other people waiting." As the curtain lowered, I lowered my head with it, my eyes fixed on Shane's face until the curtain completely closed, and he was gone.

After leaving the morgue, we met Traci in front of the U.S. Embassy. Traci led us up a steep walkway to the security entrance, where our personal items, including our passports and cellphones, were x-rayed and put in a cubbyhole. In return, we were given security clearance tags to clip on our shirts.

Once inside the embassy, we were taken to a large room, with a conference-size table, where we were given bottled water and told to wait. Soon, three men walked in: U.S. Consul Craig Bryant, FBI agent Matthew Foster, and another gentleman. As we exchanged the typical formalities, each told us how sorry he was for our loss.

At that point, Matthew Foster took charge of the meeting. After hearing a brief overview of the situation, Mr. Foster asked John and Dylan to leave the room, so he could interview Rick and me about our reaction to the suicide notes, before separately interviewing the boys. The whole process took several hours as we went through each paragraph of the alleged suicide notes, pointing out all the inconsistencies. All three men appeared engaged with what we were telling them, took notes, and asked intelligent questions. At the end of the meeting, they promised us a thorough investigation. Matthew Foster gave me his business card and told me to call or write him with any new evidence or information.

On July 9, 2012, a few days after Shane's funeral, I emailed Mr. Foster with a detailed list of the reasons why we believed Shane was murdered, including new discoveries made since our meeting at the embassy. I also included an email we received from Julius Tsai Ming, one of Shane's former supervisors at IME, who stated, "After collecting all information available, I cannot believe this is a suicide case. Actually, no one believes it or is able to detect any signs that Shane would commit suicide. I truly hope that the FBI can be involved in further investigation and recovering the true story."

To this day, I have not heard a word back from Matthew Foster. He never even acknowledged receiving my emails.

We spent the entire next day at Shane's apartment. That was the day we discovered Khal had given us a false description of how Shane allegedly hanged himself. It was the day we found and packed what we initially incorrectly identified as a computer speaker, but that we later discovered was an external hard drive.

That afternoon, we also discovered a medical report from the Psychological Wellness Center, indicating that on April 4, 2012, Shane had sought help for depression and anxiety. This report caused us to question everything. I felt like I was on a roller coaster. At one moment I was sure Shane had been murdered, but after finding this report, I thought, "Maybe he was depressed. Maybe he did take his own life."

John immediately suggested that we call Dr. Lee to discuss Shane's mental state. John got through to the office, and after talking to Dr. Lee for several minutes, he handed me the phone. I told Dr. Lee that we were told Shane committed suicide by hanging, but that there were other circumstances that indicated possible foul play. Dr. Lee told me that day, and later testified under oath, that out of all of his patients, Shane would have been the least likely to commit suicide. He stated conclusively that Shane had been anxious, but not suicidal.

Rick, in spite of my reservations, told IO Khal about Shane's visit to Dr. Lee and gave him Dr. Lee's contact information. He encouraged Khal to contact Dr. Lee, telling him that Dr. Lee had said Shane was not suicidal, but rather depressed with a high component of anxiety. Rick also gave Khal unidentified pills that we found in Shane's medicine cabinet. By this time, I completely distrusted the Singapore police, so I asked Rick why he thought it was necessary to give them this information.

Rick replied, "I'm not afraid of the truth. I want to know what happened to our son, no matter where the truth leads us. And, as inept as the Singapore police might be, they are the ones investigating Shane's death, so I want them to have all the available evidence." Rick continued, "Besides, Dr. Lee's emphatic belief that Shane was not suicidal might convince the police to actually investigate the possibility of murder."

We spent the remainder of the day in Shane's apartment with friends who came by to share their condolences and fondest memories of him. We were able to give them many of Shane's belongings. We gave three huge boxes of books that had been packed and were ready to ship to a friend and colleague from IME. We gave Shane's bike to a friend who told us he had talked to Shane about buying it. Every single one of Shane's friends said that Shane never indicated he was depressed and that they were totally shocked by his death. They all told us Shane was excited to go back to the U.S. and to be with the family again. One of them told us Shane had made arrangements to stay in his apartment for a few days before he returned to the states.

Shane's friend Margarita showed us a video of Shane, taken earlier that year, singing karaoke—one of his favorite past times. Margarita said Shane would be horrified if he knew she was playing the video for us because he was embarrassed by it. He had told her the video was not an accurate representation of his talent. But we all laughed uncontrollably, as we watched the video. It was exactly how Shane sounded—off-key, yet committed and passionate. Shane always had an elevated view of his talent as a karaoke singer. In fact, he had told his brother John that he would give up all of his degrees, if he could be the lead singer in a rock band—and he meant it! The video brought us so much joy, that we played it at Shane's memorial service.

By the time we bid farewell to Shane's friends, it was late in the evening. Lingering for no reason, we took one last look through the apartment. None of us really wanted to leave. It was comforting to be surrounded by Shane's familiar scent and his things—the packed bags, his clothes, the entertainment center with all the price tags on it, all the preparation he had done for a return trip he would never make.

By our fourth day in Singapore, we desperately wanted to go home, but there were still several arrangements that needed to be made, including another trip to the police department and a meeting with a lawyer chosen by IME to settle Shane's estate.

Cordi picked us up at our hotel to escort us to the meeting. The only notable thing about that meeting was a letter from IME that the lawyer said we needed to sign before we could receive "Shane's life insurance policy." There were so many things to sign involving Shane's estate that we didn't notice what we were signing until later. On closer examination, Rick discovered that the letter we had signed absolved IME from any wrongdoing in the death of our son. That is when we started to wonder whether the policy was really for life insurance or whether it was merely a ploy to prevent us from taking action against IME.

Our last day in Singapore, we spent mostly at the hotel. The day was filled with laughter and tears as Shane's friends continued to stop by to meet us and tell us how much they loved Shane.

That night we hosted a gathering at our hotel for about 25 of Shane's friends and colleagues, including two of Shane's former bosses. At one point, I plainly announced that I believed Shane was murdered. Patrick Lo, Shane's boss at the time of his death, responded viscerally—his face froze, he turned gray, and he walked away to make a call on his cell, which lasted at least 20 minutes. Julius Tsai Ming, Shane's former supervisor who later wrote the email I sent to

Matthew Foster, said, "I agree with you. It wasn't suicide, and you should pursue the truth."

At that time we had no idea how arduous the pursuit of truth would be—but by God's grace and abundant support from family and friends, we have found the strength to press forward and to forge our battle so that ultimately the truth might be known.

Chapter 6

IT IS WELL

G etting Shane's body home was not an easy feat. Rick handled the extensive paperwork and numerous arrangements. In spite of the difficulties and exorbitant financial cost, Traci Goins reminded us that we were fortunate Singapore had released Shane's body at all. Having since spoken to several families who lost loved ones overseas under suspicious circumstances, I believe she was right.

Finally, on Monday, July 2—the day after Shane was originally scheduled to fly home to Montana—Rick's cousin, John, picked up Shane's body from Los Angeles International Airport. We were so relieved when John called to tell us our son's body had touched U.S. soil and was on its way to the mortuary in Pomona, California.

The next morning, my sister Connie, my mom, Rick, our three remaining sons, and I went to the family's funeral home, Todd Memorial Chapel, to make the final arrangements for Shane's memorial service and burial. Rick's cousin

John met us at the mortuary. He was anguished and broken hearted. He had watched Shane grow up and knew him well.

Todd Memorial Chapel is one of Pomona's most enduring, multi-generational businesses and it has always been an important part of our lives. Shane's great-great-grandfather, Walter B. Todd, founded the mortuary in 1907. After Walter died, his son John took over. When John tragically died in a car accident at age fifty, his sons Dick (Rick's father) and Jack ran the family business, until it was eventually passed down to Jack's only son, John, and his son-in-law, Keith.

Rick worked at the mortuary when we first met in 1976 and again from 1984-1987 until he left to follow his dream of becoming an airline pilot. The boys and I would frequently visit Rick when he worked at the mortuary, where they loved to hang out in the recreation room, eat treats, and play games.

As we walked through the mortuary the somber morning following the delivery of Shane's body, I looked around and was captured by the generations of Todds whose pictures graced the walls. One picture, in particular, which caught my eye and caused me to pause, was a portrait of Dick, Shane's grandfather, whom he had affectionately named "Poppy." My mind flooded with memories of Shane and Poppy, as John ushered us into the attractive arrangement room that overlooked a flower filled, serene garden.

After making arrangements for the memorial service, John said it was time to pick out the casket, but I insisted on first seeing Shane. John placed his hand on the small of my back and gently guided me to the room where Shane's cold, still body was laying on a gurney. He encouraged me to take my time and then closed the door and left me alone with my son, while the rest of the family went to pick out the casket.

Shane's body was unclothed, covered only by a white sheet. As my eyes looked over him from head to toe, I noticed that one side of his face looked better than the other, so I rolled the gurney around to show his better side. That simple act of turning Shane's body made me feel like I was still taking care of my boy. I stroked Shane's hair, kissed his face, and thanked God for the privilege of being his mother. I was experiencing more peace in those moments, than at any other time since I had learned of my son's death. I felt like I was in a spell and was startled when, forty minutes later, John knocked and ushered the rest of the family in to see Shane.

Before we left the mortuary, Rick asked his cousin to have one of the embalmers take pictures of Shane's hands, neck, and face before they prepared him for the viewing. Rick also took Keith aside and asked whether Shane's eyes were clear. Keith said they were clear as a bell. This was significant because death by hanging usually leaves eyes bulging and blood shot.

It wasn't until I saw Shane at the viewing, lying in the open casket, that I began to realize his body was riddled with bruises. His hands were so badly bruised that the makeup could not cover the damage. Even his fingertips were bruised and there was an unexplained white line going across his fingers. There were also two noticeable bumps on his forehead. We could not see Shane's neck because he was wearing a collared shirt with his suit, but we later discovered, from the pictures taken by the embalmer, that there were scratches on his neck. Both my brother-in-law, who is a medical doctor, and our family physician commented on these bruises and bumps, believing them to be defensive wounds suggesting that Shane had fought for his life.

Rick called a pathologist who agreed to look at the body, but said that she couldn't guarantee a conclusive determination of the cause of death. At this point, I was so exhausted and emotionally drained by the conflicting accounts we were given in Singapore that I told Rick, "I can't take it anymore. I need to bury my son."

Shortly before Shane's death, Rick and I had sold our large Spanish-style house in Pomona, where we had raised our four boys, so we could move to Marion, Montana to oversee the family's newly established bed and breakfast and to start a church. In the days prior to the funeral, we were all staying at my mom's quaint house in downtown Claremont. In addition to our extended family members, who were in town for the funeral, Shane's girlfriend, Shirley, had flown in from Singapore. As we were trying to figure out where to house everybody, my dear friend Karen (who was out of town) offered her gorgeous, spacious home, in upper Claremont to us for the entire week. We gratefully accepted her generous offer. That home was an enormous blessing because it provided us with the space to be together with the ones we loved and needed most.

Two days before Shane's funeral, I sat in front of Karen's computer in her peaceful in-home art studio. I was still in shock, feeling raw and alone, as I struggled to write a memorial for Shane. I felt so inadequate, so incapable. How would it be possible to describe in one succinct page the one who had made my dream of motherhood a reality? I did the best I could and after I was done, I took my work to my niece, Christina, for editing. It was our first writing project together. Little did we know that we would later form a partnership to write our family's saga. The following is what I wrote about my son:

Shane Truman Todd, the beloved son of Rick and Mary Todd, was living in Singapore when he went home to be with our Lord on June 23, 2012.

On a gorgeous San Diego day, much to the delight of his parents, Shane Truman Todd made his splashing and dramatic entrance into the world. Shane never did things in the "normal" way. After being sucked in and out of the birth canal several times, he emerged looking like one of the Cone Heads from Saturday Night Live. We are fairly sure that this unusual birthing process is where Shane developed his extraordinary brains. At least it's the only explanation we've been able to come up with.

We moved to Pomona when Shane was three. One of the great highlights of Shane's childhood in Pomona was Ted Greene Little League. From age 13 to 23, Shane lived in Florida where he excelled in everything he put his mind to. He took first in state, fourth in the world in Science Fair, with a project he developed and named, Biological Fuel Cell utilizing Saccharomyces Cerevisiae. He continued to be an avid baseball player and won second in the state in wrestling. Shane completed his undergrad and master's at the University of Florida and went on to earn his PhD in Electrical Engineering at the University of California, Santa Barbara. After graduating, Shane had several job offers, but the one he chose was with a company in Singapore called I.M.E.

Shane accomplished many things in his short life, however, the title he took most seriously, and the one he was most proud of, was that of big brother to John, Chet, and Dylan. All the brothers looked up to Shane, and he did his best to guide them in the right direction (some were easier to guide than others). John is the one who gave Shane the name "Dubber," and he considers Shane his best friend. Chet loved being with Shane because he always felt safe when Shane was around. Dylan credits Shane for encouraging (forcing) him to go to college. Shane called Dylan everyday to help him prepare for the SATs. Without a doubt, John, Chet, and Dylan are better men for having had Shane as their big brother.

The one thing Shane hated most was when his parents would brag about his accomplishments. It is hard not to; there is a lot to brag about. By far the thing we are most proud of is not what Shane has done, but the man he had become. In the months preceding Shane's death, we spoke once a week via Skype. Shane spoke of his love for his beautiful girlfriend, Shirley. He also spoke of his recommitment to, and love for, Jesus Christ. This was the greatest gift Shane could have possibly given us. We rest in the fact that Shane is in heaven with our Lord and Savior, and we will be reunited one day in eternity. We are forever grateful and blessed to have had the privilege of being the parents of Shane Truman Todd.

The morning of Saturday, July 7, 2012, I woke up and prayed for the strength and grace to face the unthinkable task of putting my son to rest. Numerous friends and family members came from all over the country to show their love and respect for Shane and to bring comfort to us. The funeral was beautiful. Our pastor, Glenn Gunderson, did a magnificent job honoring Shane and encouraging those at the service to remember the words of Romans 8:28: "And we know that in all things God works for the good of those who love him, who have been called according to his purpose." Glenn stressed that this life is only a dot on the infinite line of eternity and that we should live in view of the line, not the dot.

One of the most poignant moments of the service was when each one of Shane's brothers got up to speak. Dylan spoke first, then Chet, and finally John, who introduced a short video of Shane's life. All the boys would agree that Chet's tearful words summed up their sentiments well: "My brothers are sacred to me. Our bond cannot be broken by death. Though Shane spent most of his adult life either on the opposite side of the state, country, or world, knowing he was there gave me great comfort, and I always had hope of seeing him again. Shane was our leader and our protector. My hope continues, and I know that it will not be long before I get to see my brother's smiling face again."

During the service, Rick recounted the story of Horatio Spafford, who—after he experienced the loss of his young son to scarlet fever, the destruction of most of his wealth in the Great Chicago Fire, and then the tragic death of his four daughters with the sinking of an ocean liner in the North Atlantic—penned the well-known hymn, "It Is Well with My Soul." Since Shane's death, this powerful hymn has encouraged me not to be defeated by the sorrow, despair, and evil of this world, but to find my purpose and fight my battle in view of the glorious promise of eternity.

Chapter 7

THE DISCOVERY

Shortly after Shane's funeral, Rick and I returned to Montana and began a letter writing campaign to our elected officials, the Department of Homeland Security, the FBI, the CIA, and various media outlets requesting an investigation into our son's death. On the morning of Sunday, July 22, 2012, as we were sitting at the dining room table in our apartment writing letters, Rick suddenly looked up with an expression that said, "I can't believe I didn't think of this before." He exclaimed, "Mary, you know that 'speaker' we found in Shane's apartment, I think it might actually be an external hard drive!"

Rick ran to the back bedroom and began rummaging through the bag of Shane's things, until he finally found the "speaker." He returned to the dining room table and eagerly plugged it into his computer. As Shane's files began to appear on the screen, he yelped in astonishment, "Oh my gosh, this is Shane's backup hard drive!" Remembering what my brother Richard had warned about handling computer evidence, Rick quickly unplugged the hard drive and said,

"This could be huge. Call Richard and ask him how to contact the computer forensic guy he told you about."

When I told Richard about Rick's discovery, he immediately put me in touch with his friend Ashraf Massoud, a computer forensic expert, who worked for DataChasers. Ashraf was friendly and professional, and told us he would be happy to examine the hard drive if we could get it to him in Southern California. Rick, knowing the possible significance of the hard drive's contents, did not want to send it through the mail. Fortunately, our son John agreed to make the two-leg flight to Ontario, California to hand deliver the hard drive to Ashraf that same day.

Ashraf warned us that the analysis of the hard drive could take time, so as Rick and I waited a couple weeks in suspense to hear what he discovered, we continued writing letters. At that point we had no idea what kind of evidence Ashraf would find, so we only wrote about our conversations with Shane before his death, the fake suicide notes, and the defensive wounds on Shane's body.

A few people who responded to our concerns tried to be helpful, but most simply placated us. A staffer from California Congressman David Dreier's office called, listened attentively to our story, and promised to look into the matter, but eventually stopped answering or returning our calls. Jennifer, from Montana Senator Jon Tester's office, did her best to accommodate us. She always took our phone calls, always forwarded our messages to Senator Tester, and was extremely kind. But, at that point, Tester's office offered no help.

During this time, a long-time family friend, Jenny, who had lived in Jakarta, Indonesia for some years, connected us with two reporters whom she thought might be interested in assisting us. One of the reporters, Jeremy Wagstaff, worked for *Reuters* in Singapore. The other was a Pulitzer Prize winning investigative reporter named Ray Bonner. We were encouraged because both men seemed eager to hear our story and help us uncover the truth.

Our personal communications with Jeremy Wagstaff began on July 19, when he emailed Jenny explaining that he was interested in Shane's death because it might "have defense and technology ramifications." He did caution, however, that such cases were "very hard to investigate in Singapore."

After we emailed Wagstaff to introduce ourselves and provide an overview of our situation, he replied with the following email requesting more information:

Jul 20, 2012

Mary,

I've spoken to one of the people mentioned in the emails who was very helpful. It would be helpful to me if you have any documentation of your interactions with the police, and any photos—including Shane's supposed suicide note, the wounds to his body, the crime scene etc.

I'd also be grateful for any chronologies or timelines, notes etc. you may have of the last few months of Shane's life and your visit to Singapore. I've started compiling a chronology myself, but the more I'm able to add to it the clearer the picture I can build. Any emails etc., however innocuous, or dates/times of phone calls, anything that may trigger a memory, would be helpful at this point.

Right now I don't have an awful lot to go on, but I'll keep talking to as many people as possible to see whether I'm able to uncover anything. I'll try to keep you updated insofar as my position as a journalist allows.

I can't promise that anything will come out of my research, but I'll try.

Best,

Jeremy

Rick and I were ecstatic that Wagstaff was interested in our story. We needed all the help we could get, so I immediately sent him everything he had requested: the suicide notes, the pictures of the defensive wounds, a timeline, a description of our interaction with the police, and Shane's emails from the several months prior to his death.

Among the many emails I sent to Wagstaff, I included the following letter that Shane had written less than two weeks before his death to Knowles Electronics (one of the U.S. companies he had applied to work for). This letter became more significant once we learned what was on Shane's hard drive. It also gives insight into Shane's upbeat personality and optimistic spirit.

The letter begins with Shane's enthusiasm for the prospect of working for Knowles Electronics.

June 11, 2012

Dear Knowles Electronics,

I am very excited to apply for the MEMS (Micro Electro-mechanical Systems) engineer position at Knowles electronics. This job scope looks interesting and challenging and directly aligns with my previous experience and future career aspirations. I have always been someone who gets excited by implementing new ideas. When I have a problem that needs to be solved, I think about it constantly—at work and also when I am away from work. And if I think of a solution, I will often times stop whatever I'm doing, get in the car and go to work to try it out. This is a passion that results from doing what I love to do and I want to bring this passion to help your team accomplish great things.

For the last year and a half I've worked on the MEMS devices and GaN power electronics at the Institute of Microelectronics (IME) in Singapore. Working with IME has been an extremely rewarding experience where I have had the opportunity to work with engineers from all over the world. My experience working with international teams has prepared me to successfully engage with the overseas manufacturing facilities as outlined in the job scope. I am now ready to return to the U.S. to continue my career at home, and the opportunity to work as a MEMS engineer at Knowles Electronics is the kind of challenge I am looking for.

The body of the letter describes the scope and highly technical aspects of Shane's experience.

To meet the diverse device requirements and multidisciplinary nature of MEMS work, a proficient MEMS engineer must be well versed in all aspects of the MEMS product cycle and have experience with a wide variety of devices. I have experience with the design, modeling, simulation, fabrication and characterization of MEMS devices including switches microseive filters, multi-dimensional micromirrors, micromachined transmission line circuits, Fabry-Perot optical spectral meters, electrothermal actuators, and piezoelectric actuators. For device design, I have used multiple layout editors such as L-edit, ADS, and Cadence and combine this with atypical models and device simulations for design optimization. I developed analytical models for predicting device behavior in electrothermo micromirrors, micromachined transmission lines, and nanoelectromechanical switches. I have used simulation software such as Coventor and Silvaco for device simulations.

My processing experience has been in both manufacturing and research facilities. My recent fabrication work at IME was conducted on an 8" line where I worked on the process development of nanoelectromechanical switches, microsieve filters, and GaN power electronic devices. In graduate school at UC Santa Barbara and the University of Florida I worked in processes for micro-machined transmission line circuits and multidimensional micromirrors. I also worked in a CMOS manufacturing line at AMD as a process engineer intern. I've done extensive work in device characterization where I have used equipment such as parameter analyzers, network analyzers, optical profilers, laser vibrometers, and thermal images for device measurement.

The letter concludes with Shane's self-assessment.

As a result of my efforts and experience in MEMS I have first author journal publications and one granted U.S. patent. This solid portfolio of experience allows me to quickly adapt to challenges that a MEMS engineer faces and gives me the confidence that I can successfully pursue new MEMS projects.

Complementing my technical strengths in background, I bring a set of personal qualities that contribute to successful team projects.

I am a highly motivated individual who works hard to complete tasks and accomplish goals to make a project successful. I can get along with all kinds of people and I know the importance of maintaining good personal relationships with coworkers in order to achieve successful results and contribute to a healthy work environment. I have excellent communication skills and I pay a great deal of attention to being clear and concise when explaining ideas and results to other people. I'm excited for the opportunity to return to the United States and work at Knowles Electronics as a MEMS Engineer developing next-generation devices. Please contact me anytime if you have questions.

Best regards,
Shane Todd

I will never forget the afternoon of July 26, 2012, when Rick, the boys, and I were enjoying a gorgeous afternoon at the lake house. Still reeling from the shock of all we'd been through and the reality of life without Shane, we found consolation in each other's company as we shared tears and laughter while relaxing in the Jacuzzi. When my fingers started to look like prunes, I excused myself to go in the house and check my emails. As I opened my inbox, I was excited to see an email from Jeremy Wagstaff. My hopes, however, were quickly dashed. I stood frozen, the blood drained from my face, and I felt the urge to throw up, as my eyes scanned his email:

Mary,

Thanks for sending me this information. I will continue to talk to people and hopefully we'll hear something about the autopsy at some point, but, at the moment, I believe it was suicide because according to my conversations with colleagues (who have preferred to remain anonymous for obvious reasons, so I can't share the notes I have, unfortunately, at least for now). The following may not make for comfortable reading.

The suicide notes, which I showed to colleagues who knew him as well as anyone appears to have [known him] in Singapore, "sounded like Shane." He was or had been depressed, according to them, about several things and he expressed them all in the notes.

Most particularly, he was having problems coming to terms with a sense of failure at quitting IME. He spent quite a bit of time alone since handing in his notice and this may have worsened his mood. While sometimes he could be outgoing and lively, his colleagues remember him being withdrawn on several occasions and yet having difficulty expressing the reasons why.

He had been looking for work in the U.S. and while there may be information to the contrary, it wasn't clear he had a job waiting for him back in the U.S.—at least one he was looking forward to. The process of looking for work was getting him down: on one occasion he dressed up and prepared for a video interview via Skype only for the company in question not to call.

I'm not clear about the state of his relationship with Shirley. She was not with him on the Friday night after his farewell lunch, and it seems they didn't have plans to see each other until going to church together on Sunday. As far as his colleagues know he had no plans to see anyone else in the interim. But his colleagues' attest to the feelings he expressed in the suicide note that he was aware he was not always good company for her.

He had spoken of wanting to stay on in Singapore and Asia but could find no way of doing so without adding to his sense of failure. He had expressed a desire to return to the original team he joined when he first started at IME, reversing his mistake of moving upstairs, but he was troubled by what people at IME would think of him if he did so. He did not seem able to shake of this feeling, despite his colleagues saying it didn't matter.

He worked extremely hard at IME, perhaps overly so. There were two kinds of people at IME, one colleague told me: those who let the place get to them and those who didn't. Some found it hard not to take personally having to present their work to others and having it judged, sometimes harshly. Others didn't care so much. They saw it as just a place to work for a while and then move on. (There's no question the place is dysfunctional and has a high turnover, but I can't find any obvious evidence of malfeasance or IP theft, at least in Shane's case.)

As I mentioned in the last note, the other factors which point to suicide are:

- The extreme complexity of any plausible murder conspiracy. Those involved would need to have known him in order to gain entry and overcome him without any visible sign of struggle, would have either forced him to write the notes or have written them themselves, would have had to have been confident he had no further appointments so they would not be disturbed, and would have had to have already prepared the method by which they would make it appear as a suicide. Not impossible, of course, but the less obvious explanation.
- The lack of an obvious motive or suspect. Beyond the conversations he had with you, I've found no evidence yet of a clear reason why someone would want him dead, and who would have the means to do so. Furthermore, if they went to such lengths, they would surely have removed any possible storage devices or evidence that may link them to the murder, or wiped them, and yet the police have the laptop, and you have the USB and external drives. Either they were supremely confident there was nothing on there before they arrived, or they had time to look through all of them to be sure.
- I admit I've not looked more deeply into the method of his death, nor have we had a chance to go through his emails and other data. But the above, in my view, doesn't yet add up to suspicious circumstances.

I hope this is of some help. I know it may appear superficial, and appears to contradict a lot of the things that persuaded you to explore your suspicions, and I don't expect this to change your mind. I just wanted to lay out, in response to your request, my findings so far. I'm sorry that I can't share the details of the interviews I've had but that was at their request. I'd also be grateful if you didn't share this email with others; it's written for you in confidence in my personal capacity.

Best,
Jeremy

As I read the email, I could not hide my horror: "How could we have so misread Shane's colleagues and their view of our son?" I was particularly stunned because even after we left Singapore, Shane's friends had continued to send us messages saying how shocked and saddened they were by his death. The following are just a few of the many notes we received:

- *A. R. K.—NanoElectronics*
  My relationship with Shane was more as a friend than as a professional colleague. His passion for research was very evident from his work at the same time he took some time to follow his other passions such as kite surfing. He was a fun loving and easy going guy. All I can say is Shane was an epitome for the adage "work hard play harder." I will miss this friend of mine....
- *T. K.—Sensors & Actuators Microsystems*
  Shane was a really polite and respectful person. He would acknowledge and praise someone whenever someone did a great thing. I would swing my lanyard with the IME pass towards the door scanner and Shane would go: Hey! That's an awesome trick you did just now dude!

  I was quite surprised as it was just something I would do in the morning to clock my attendance in IME, but Shane would drop me the compliment for that action, whereas other people would think of it as a childish act.

  He also respected everyone no matter how small their title. In my department, I was only an assistant lab officer, however, when Shane was showing the probe station in my lab to his understudy student, he would address me as the 'lab manager'…

Well, I cannot describe fully in words everything. I just know that I gained a friend when Shane came to IME, not a colleague, but a friend indeed…

- *W. X.—NanoElectronics*

Actually I was very shocked when I heard that news since Shane was a very friendly, active and optimistic man…

When we started to work at IME, we sat at different stories. But after some time, Shane transferred internally to lead a new project and his new working cubicle was quite close to mine, so that we became neighbors again. After that, we had more chances to meet, and every time he would show me a friendly and charming smile, actually not only to me, but to all colleagues around him… So, all of us were really shocked and felt deeply sorry when we heard that disastrous news…

- *G. H.—Interconnection & Advanced Packaging*

I'll always remember Shane as a true gentle giant—from his booming voice to his wide smile, stretching from ear to ear, Shane was hard to miss in any room. I knew him best in moments of play, whether it's in a boisterous game of laser-tag, where Shane would lead the charge up a hill (or gallantly provide cover for his team-mates), or in beach volleyball, playing his heart out for his team with many saving dives (and accumulating battle scars to show for it). In dragon-boating, he'd be at the head of the boat, setting the pace for the rest of us. It was clear to the rest of us that he took his responsibilities seriously and that above all, we could count on him. In many ways, Shane was simply, outstanding. I am truly sorry for your loss of a wonderful soul.

We later asked one of Shane's closest friends at IME why Wagstaff's account was so different from what we had personally heard from Shane's co-workers. He told us that when Wagstaff requested an interview with a couple of Shane's co-workers, IME chose two people to speak to him who had not worked with Shane and did not know him well.

Although our personal communication with Jeremy Wagstaff was short-lived, he later became a bizarre and important part of our story as he spent the rest of the year aggressively trying to prove Shane committed suicide. Ray Bonner, on the other hand, ended up being a godsend. He was the only one who took the time to really listen to and investigate our allegations, our evidence, and our suspicions.

Ray, a self-proclaimed "crusty old guy," began his career practicing law and then teaching at the University of California, Davis School of Law, before becoming an investigative reporter and foreign correspondent. Ray has always had an innate hatred of injustice and spent much of his career fighting against it. He took ten years to meticulously write, *Anatomy of Injustice*, the powerful and poignant analysis of a grievously mishandled murder case that put an innocent man on death row.

At first Ray, was bothered and puzzled by Shane's death, but was not convinced that Shane was murdered. However, the more Ray learned about our son's death, the more intrigued and outraged he became over how our case had been handled by the police. Over the next few months, we spent hours emailing Ray, sending him information, Skyping with him, and connecting him with Ashraf, the forensic expert, as he prepared to break our story to the international media.

On August 5, 2012, much sooner than we expected, we received Ashraf's preliminary report on his analysis2 of Shane's external Seagate hard drive. According to the report, it appeared Shane had performed a backup of files located in the folder C:\IME on Friday morning, June 22, before his farewell luncheon. However, the most astonishing news was that the hard drive showed activity on it after Shane's death. Ashraf's analysis revealed the following:

- On Saturday, June 23, 2012, between 3:40am and 3:42am five folders containing IME related data were accessed, meaning they were opened

2   Ashraf Massoud's complete analysis of the external Seagate hard drive is included in the appendix.

and viewed for whatever reason but the contents of the folders were not changed.

- Of even greater significance, is the fact that no other user initiated activity was recorded on the hard drive throughout the remainder of June 23, 2012 through June 27, 2012, until four folders and one file were accessed on June 27, 2012, between 8:38:39pm and 8:40:28pm, three days after Shane's body was discovered in his apartment.

- Of real concern is that the Microsoft temporary file called "~$characterization result to veeco.pptx" was deleted within that time frame. Although temporary files are usually automatically deleted, this file appears to have been manually deleted.

While we were shocked that someone was accessing Shane's external hard drive after his death, we had no idea what any of these files meant, so Rick contacted one of Shane's colleagues from IME. He told Rick that the files were associated with the work Shane had been doing with a Chinese company called Huawei. Rick then asked him what kind of company Huawei was. The colleague informed him that Huawei was a telecommunications company. When Rick asked if he thought that Huawei could be involved with Shane's death, the colleague responded that it would be highly unlikely because, "Huawei is benign; it's like Cisco."

Rick and I were confused. If this Chinese company were benign, then why were files associated with it accessed on Shane's hard drive after his death? Who had opened these files and what were they looking for? We also began to realize that this might be the same Chinese company that Shane had expressed concerns about, but we still couldn't understand why a company likened to Cisco would pose a threat to U.S. security and our son.

Sometime later, however, several friends told us about a "60 Minutes" segment that had aired on October 7, 2012 on the Chinese telecommunication giant Huawei. Far from portraying Huawei as benign, the segment explained that the company had been the subject of a year-long investigation by the House Intelligence Committee and had developed a daunting reputation for industrial espionage with "murky connections to the Chinese government."

Rick and I knew this was extremely significant, so we immediately asked Ashraf to search Shane's hard drive for the following keywords: Huawei, GaN, U.S. export/import control law, and Patrick Lo. This process—the discovery of that hard drive and the results of Ashraf's research—transformed our personal tragedy into a mystery worthy of international attention.

Chapter 8

THE DREAM

The discovery of Shane's external hard drive was encouraging, and even exciting on some levels, because it got us closer to the truth. But it didn't make our lives any easier. In fact, each day was a battle as Rick and I struggled to learn how to live with our "new normal"—sitting in our apartment, alone together, day after day, feeling the weight of being the sole investigators into the death of our son. We were crushed and somewhat in denial. Often we would look at each other and ask, "Is this our life?" The death of a child does strange things to people. Rick's and my mostly conflict-free relationship became more and more strained. We grieved differently, and our tempers were fragile, creating fertile ground for misunderstandings and arguments. However, because we were both one hundred percent committed to our marriage, we did our best to try to understand each other and extend one another grace.

For the first year after Shane's death, sleep for me was fleeting. In fact, there were many nights it was so elusive and fitful, I'm not sure I slept at all. One thought keeping me up night after night was that of Shane's final moments. As hard as I tried not to think about it, my mind always returned to the "what happened," and "what if" questions that plague those in tragic circumstances like ours. I was haunted by thoughts such as: "What exactly happened to Shane?" "How long did he fight for his life?" "Did he call out my name?" "Was the battle painful?" "How long did he suffer?" "Why didn't Shane fly home the minute he thought his life was in danger?" "Why didn't I take Shane seriously and fly to Singapore when he told me he felt his life was being threatened?" I tried everything to stop these relentless questions—I prayed, I counted backwards, I read books, I surfed the internet—but nothing worked. Night after night, my mind was tormented.

Rick and I desperately needed to get away, to escape, anything to get our minds off our situation. Yet in September of 2012, when it came time for the Pomona First Baptist (PFB) Pastors' Retreat in Lake Tahoe, we didn't want to go. It was too soon after Shane's death, and we couldn't imagine putting a smile on our faces and being with all those people. In spite of our misgivings, however, we felt obligated to attend because PFB had already paid our way.

Rick and I were invited to the pastor's retreat because we had started a PFB satellite church in our airplane hangar in Montana. Our decision to start this church, which has become an integral part of our lives, can be traced all the way back to 2002 when I had an opportunity to speak to students during a chapel service at Azusa Pacific University (APU) in Southern California. As I chatted with some of these students, I felt drawn to them, and since they responded well to me, I began to consider becoming a campus pastor.

At the time, my only qualifications were an associate's degree in early childhood education, years of teaching Bible study, and motherhood. So, I decided to go back to school to complete my undergraduate degree in Christian leadership. After continuing on to earn a master's in organizational leadership from APU, I was hired as an assistant campus pastor. My job was to spend time with students and help them find direction in their lives through biblical counseling. To augment my qualifications, I also went through the process of becoming a licensed pastor with PFB.

After three wonderful years at APU, I moved to Marion, Montana to oversee the construction of our bed and breakfast located on an airstrip, where we had already built an airplane hangar with an apartment above. I began working with Murphy Wagar, our contractor, whom I called "the slave driver." Not only did he have me faux painting vaulted walls and ceilings on a scissor lift with his wife Michelle, but he also pushed me daily to make decisions about paint colors, bathroom fixtures, lighting, wood flooring, carpeting, and on and on. I would plead, "Murphy, please give me a little time to think about it."

With a pleasant grin on his face, Murphy would remind me, "We're on a schedule here." Even though I gave Murphy a hard time, I loved working with him, and so did everyone else.

Every day during the building project, Murphy would make the same observation about one or more of his workers: "That guy needs God; his life is a mess."

And every day I would reply, "Murphy, everyone needs God—we're all a mess."

One day I asked why no one in the area went to church. Murphy spouted off several excuses, one of which was that nobody wanted to drive all the way into Kalispell, a 60-mile roundtrip. Without really thinking it through, I asked Murphy, "If we started a church in our airplane hangar, do you think anyone would come?" Murphy responded affirmatively.

Rick ended up loving the idea of starting a church, so we flew down to Southern California to run the idea by Peter Torry, the executive pastor at PFB. Within nine months of that meeting, Peter had arranged for the church technician to come to Montana and wire our hangar, complete with a sound system, overhead projector and screen for Pastor Gunderson to preach via satellite every Sunday to "The Hangar Church." Murphy became our head elder, and his wife Michelle became our Sunday school superintendent. Since our first Sunday evening service in 2010, we've only missed opening our hangar door one Sunday night—the night of June 24, 2012, when we were on our way to Singapore.

The pastor's retreat in Lake Tahoe ended up providing the reprieve Rick and I so desperately needed. We had a wonderful time of fellowship, encouragement, and prayer. But the most significant event was a dream I had in the middle of our second night there. I've never had a dream like it before or since. It was more real and vibrant than anything I'd ever experienced. I dreamt that I was back in Southern California in my kitchen cooking, when suddenly the outside door opened and in walked Shane wearing his typical shorts and T-shirt. In my dream, I knew Shane was dead, but he looked radiant and alive. My face lit up at the sight of his glowing smile, and I gasped, "Shane, is that you?"

He responded, "Yes, it's me."

I couldn't believe my eyes and asked again, "Shane, is it really you?"

Shane excitedly replied, "Yes, Mom, it's really me!"

I immediately ran into his open arms and hugged his huge body. I could feel his beard on my face. I could smell his breath. I touched his hair. We just kept kissing and hugging, until someone walked in the door, and Shane was gone.

That dream fundamentally changed something in my heart. I woke up in the morning and told Rick about seeing Shane and how beautiful and joyful he looked. From that point on, I have not worried or spent any time thinking about how Shane died. All those thoughts that tormented me at night disappeared. That dream also enabled me to encourage my other sons to try to move beyond their grief. One day, Dylan told me that he felt guilty because he had gone a full day without feeling sad about Shane. I told him, with confidence, never to feel such guilt because Shane is in heaven, where there is no mourning or pain.

That vision of Shane was an amazing gift that I will treasure forever. It was also what I needed to continue the grueling search for the truth about what had ended my son's time on earth.

Rick and I came home from that pastor's retreat with a renewed sense of purpose and we continued to devote ourselves to the investigation. Ray Bonner, the investigative reporter, also became more involved in the case after Rick sent him an email from David Sherrer, the president of Nuvotronics, the Virginia company that had offered Shane a job upon his return to the United States. Responding to a question about the technology Shane was working on at IME, David Sherrer wrote,

I don't know any specifics of what Shane was working on at the Institute in Singapore except for GaN HEMT on Silicon as outlined in his resume. Historically he was also working on low loss microwave transmission lines... GaN devices and low loss transmission lines put together can be the basis for creating solid state microwave power modules and amplifiers that are used in jammers, phased arrays, towed decoys, and other modules and systems for next generation space, aerospace, and defense. The combination of these technologies, depending on how they are used, could provide differentiating capability against legacy technology, and certainly our government has invested substantially in GaN. [emphasis added] If I were to speculate, if you have good reason to suspect foul play, I might look into any connections [of] who could have wanted Shane to work in, or for, a firm doing GaN or GaN based modules for Chinese national interests...

In October 2012, Rick and I took a road trip, a favorite shared activity. The trip was relaxing and fun, and it gave us the opportunity to stop by and see our dear friends Andy and Tina Kasanicky in Colorado. Andy was an old friend from when we lived in Boca Raton, Florida where he was our children's junior high youth leader. He hung out with our family so much that I often referred to him as my fifth son. The minute Andy heard of Shane's death, he offered to fly to Montana to run the bed and breakfast, so our entire family could be together in Southern California for Shane's funeral.

During our visit with the Kasanikys, we received a phone call from Rick's sister Mary. Her husband Hal had talked with Dr. Edward Adlestein, Chief of Pathology at Harry S. Truman Veterans' Hospital in Columbia, Missouri, asking him if there were clear ways to differentiate between suicide and murder. Dr. Adelstein had conducted more than 25 autopsies on individuals who had committed suicide and died by asphyxiation from a ligature around the neck. After hearing about Shane and the circumstances surrounding his death, Dr. Adelstein volunteered, without charge, to review Shane's autopsy and toxicology reports and the pictures of his body that were taken at the mortuary.

We sent Dr. Adelstein all of this information and then called to discuss his analysis. Dr. Adelstein was direct and professional. He began by telling us that when he had agreed to look at the evidence and give his opinion on the manner of Shane's death, he warned Hal that we might not like his findings because most cases like Shane's are typically found to be death by suicide. He continued, however, to explain that after examining Shane's autopsy report and seeing the pictures of Shane's defensive wounds, he could only conclude that Shane was murdered.

Dr. Adelstein listed several reasons why he believed Shane's death was a homicide: Shane's lung weight recorded in the autopsy report meant he died within 30 seconds, while death by hanging takes four to eight minutes. All the scratches and chafing around Shane's neck indicated Shane had tried to get his fingers under a wire, possibly explaining the white line across his bruised fingers. Dr. Adelstein thus deduced that Shane was killed by at least two men, one who came from behind Shane to put the wire around his neck, and the other who was fighting Shane from the front. Being attacked from the front would explain the two bumps on Shane's forehead—Shane was a rugby player throughout college and grad school, and the head butt was one of his signature defensive moves.

In the report[3] that Dr. Adelstein later sent us, he drew the following conclusions:

In summary, based on the information I have received, the autopsy findings and the pictures provided, I would suggest the following sequence of events that led to Shane Todd's death, which I believe to be a homicide.

- He engaged in a fight as evidenced by the blunt trauma to both hands.
- He was killed by an encircling ligature (garroting) and death occurred quickly.
- After death, he was suspended by a broader base ligature in an attempt to secure the original thinner ligature.

---

3   Dr. Adelstein's report is available at www.justice4shanetodd.com.

On October 9, armed with this new assessment from Dr. Adelstein, Rick and I immediately started writing emails to the State Department, the Singapore Police Force, the FBI, and our elected officials, attaching Dr. Adelstein's report and pleading for a murder investigation. Rick also sent the following email to Detective Khal and his superior:

Dear Khal and Gurcharn:

Mary and I had Dr. Adelstein, a respected pathologist in the United States, review pictures of Shane's body and his autopsy report. Please review his investigative report on the cause of Shane's death.

In light of what Shane told us in the months prior to his death, the sensitive nature of his work in regards to the Veeco k465i system GaN-on-Si and the transfer of its technology to the Chinese, I am asking you to change your focus from a suicide investigation to a murder investigation. There needs to be a collaboration on the forensic computer evidence that we have from Shane's back up hard drive and what you have on the Shane's computers. Mary and I would like to fly to Singapore to meet with you, the FBI, and the Department of Homeland Security, if they are available there. Please inform us when we can meet, so we can make arrangements to fly to Singapore.

Yours Truly,
Rick Todd

Rick and I waited anxiously to hear back from the investigating officers, only to be disappointed once again when Khal responded with a report written by a Singaporean pathologist, Dr. Wee Keng Poh, who denied and rebutted Dr. Adelstein's findings. In his two-page report, Dr. Poh stated that Dr. Adelstein "does not know what are the differences between the autopsy findings of hanging as opposed to ligature strangulation (garroting)." He also claimed there were no scratches on Shane's neck, saying, "In ligature strangulation, because there is often a struggle for life, one can expect to find fingernail scratches on the front and side of the neck. There were none." Later Dr. Poh testified under oath that the bruises on Shane's hands were not bruises, but were from levity (blood pooling). He also denied the clearly visible bumps on Shane's head.[4]

When Rick called Dr. Adelstein to tell him about the Singapore pathologist's rebuttal of his report, Dr. Adelstein said that he was confident in his conclusion about how Shane died, and that he did not know of a pathologist, in his or her right mind, who would call those bruises levity. In fact, according to Dr. Adelstein, three other pathologists on his staff had come to the same conclusion of homicide in looking through the reports and photos.

In spite of Dr. Adelstein's encouraging findings, we realized that we had been naïve to think that we could get a serious investigation into the death of our son. For some unknown reason, the Singapore Police could not be persuaded to even consider the possibility of murder.

---

4 We later learned that the Singapore Police were distributing what seem to be a doctored set of photographs. See the photographs at www.justice4shanetodd.com for a comparison of those distributed by the police with those taken at the mortuary.

Chapter 9

THE BLATANT LIE

hortly after we sent Dr. Adlestein's report to the FBI and the U.S. Embassy, Traci Goins, Vice Consul to the U.S. Embassy, emailed to ask whether we had heard from the Singapore police. She also explained that the FBI office in Singapore had not yet opened a case into Shane's death because they have no independent jurisdiction in Singapore and the Singaporean government had refused to invite them to assist with the investigation.[5] This took us by complete surprise. During our first trip to Singapore, FBI agent Mathew Foster led us to believe that the FBI was going to follow up on our allegations of murder—which is why we had continued to send information and evidence. We also thought it strange that, although an American had died under extremely suspicious circumstances, Singapore was refusing help from the best investigative bureau in the world.

---

5   As reported in the *Financial Times*, the FBI in Washington later confirmed that the agency
     had twice offered its assistance, notably in forensics, but that the Singapore police had
     refused it. Raymond Bonner and Christine Spolar, "Death in Singapore," *Financial Times*,
     February 15, 2013.

As Rick and I considered our next move, we concluded that we should fly to Singapore and meet face to face with the Singapore police, the U.S. ambassador, and IME. We were convinced that if we directly confronted each of these parties with the pictures of Shane's defensive wounds, Dr. Adelstein's findings, and the computer forensic report, they would not be able to deny the concrete evidence of foul play. We also believed that the potential national security implications of Shane's involvement with Huawei might convince the FBI to pursue their own investigation.

While we were often discouraged by the lack of response from our elected officials, Homeland Security, the State Department, and especially the FBI, every so often we would receive encouraging news and would feel like we were finally getting somewhere. For example, on October 18, 2012, we received a call from Jennifer at Senator Tester's office, informing us that the State Department, Homeland Security, and Immigration and Customs Enforcement were closely watching our case. Jennifer also offered to set up a phone meeting with the U.S. ambassador to Singapore. Calls like that always gave us hope that our government was going to take our son's death seriously.

On November 11, 2012, Ashraf Massoud finished his official forensic report detailing what he had discovered on Shane's external hard drive. As soon as we received the report, Rick forwarded it to Craig Bryant, Traci Goins, Matthew Foster, Senator Tester's office, and Ray Bonner.[6] Ashraf's report inspired Ray to continue his investigation, and about a week after receiving it, he informed us that a very prestigious and influential magazine was interested in publishing our story and that he was heading to Singapore to conduct interviews. We later found out that the magazine Ray was referring to was the *Financial Times*, one of the largest worldwide publications. We were thrilled! From that point on, we emailed or spoke with Ray on a daily basis, as he began to immerse himself in Shane's life.

---

6   Ashraf Massoud's report is included in Appendix B.

In response to Ray's many questions, I told him about Shane's love of sports and how he played baseball through high school and then joined the wrestling team during the "off season" to maintain and develop his strength. I told Ray that during Shane's second year at University of Florida, he was offered a wrestling scholarship to Stanford, but turned it down because he was happy at Florida and didn't want to leave. I also told him that Shane played rugby throughout college and grad school because he was drawn to the intensity and camaraderie of the sport. In fact, many of Shane's rugby friends from college and grad school traveled from all over the country to attend his funeral.

I also informed Ray that Shane was an avid learner, who was particularly gifted in math and science, and that, as a high school student, he received first place in the Florida State Engineering Fair for creating a biofuel cell by extracting energy through the fermentation process. I explained how during college Shane became even more interested in scientific research and development. After completing his masters at the University of Florida, Shane chose to pursue a PhD at the University of California, Santa Barbara because it has one of the best photonics departments in the world, and of course he wanted to be near his family and the beach.

After receiving my information and viewing a video of Shane's funeral, Ray replied to say how deeply touched he was and that Shane was indeed an extraordinary man. He also determined that our trip to Singapore was imperative and agreed to meet us there, so he could report on all of our encounters.

In preparation for our trip to Singapore, Rick and I began corresponding with U.S. Consul Craig Bryant. In my first email to Craig, I explained that, in spite of all of the evidence we had sent to the Singapore police, they were not responding to our request for a meeting. I asked for Craig's advice and direction, and if it would be possible to speak personally with the ambassador when we arrived in Singapore.

Craig replied with the following:

Dear Mrs. Todd:

At this time, there has been no final determination as to whether the death of your son was a suicide or homicide. We have urged the Singapore police to conduct a thorough investigation of all the circumstances surrounding your son's death, and they have assured me that they will do so. It's my understanding that you have sent the police the report prepared by the independent pathologist, so they have that additional evidence. If there is any additional evidence you would like to provide to the police, please send it to me and I will ensure they receive it.

When the police have completed the investigation, a coroner's inquest will be conducted. I have no reason to believe that the police are attempting to cover up the cause of Shane's death, or that they are ignoring any of the information that you have provided them...

Craig concluded by saying that he and Traci had taken the lead role at the embassy with respect to Shane's death, and that they had requested a meeting with the police for an update on the investigation. Craig later informed us that he would arrange for us to speak with the ambassador and that the police had finally agreed to meet with us. He said that the police specifically requested that we provide them with Shane's external hard drive and his "EZ Link" metro card.

Although we were grateful that Craig had managed to set up appointments with the ambassador and the police, his statement that the police would do a thorough investigation and that we should continue to send them information was disappointing. "We have sent them enough," we complained to Craig. "It's time for them to perform!"

We arrived in Singapore early Saturday morning, December 8, 2012, and spent Sunday visiting with Shane's girlfriend, Shirley. Our first scheduled meeting was with Craig and Traci at the U.S. Embassy at 11:00 Monday morning.[7] Traci was her normal warm, engaging self. Craig, on the other

---

7   Each evening in Singapore, I would recap the events of the day in an email to family members and close friends. These emails have been invaluable in helping me precisely

hand, seemed cold and aloof. He did not display an ounce of sympathy or compassion. He wasn't even polite.

Rick and I had no idea what Craig and Traci wanted to discuss. After being ushered into a small office, we sat waiting for someone to break the ice. Finally, Craig started off by demanding to know why we had not given the hard drive to the Singapore police like he had requested, emphasizing that they were our only hope. We responded that the police, thus far, had not been truthful or forthright, and that, based on our experience, we did not trust their integrity or ability. Craig was enraged, "Are you saying the Singapore police are corrupt? That's a serious charge!"

I responded, "My son's death is serious!"

Rick quickly interjected and explained that we were not claiming outright corruption, but we certainly believed they had mishandled the investigation. After all, they had not given us an accurate description of the scene in Shane's apartment, and they had not even dusted for fingerprints or taken photographs until after Shane's body had been taken down from the door.

While we were surprised by Craig's angry demeanor, nothing could have prepared us for what came next. We sat flabbergasted as Traci informed us that the police were claiming that IO Khal, the officer assigned to Shane's case, had found Shane's external hard drive in his apartment, that he was the one who accessed it after Shane's death, and that he had given it to us.

Rick and I were incensed at this blatant lie. We began to ask obvious questions such as: "Why would a rookie police officer have the right to access our son's computer after his death? Not to mention, out of the thousands of files on the drive, how would he know to look up the sensitive files involving Huawei?"

Traci explained that Khal told them that he had taken the computer attached to the hard drive back to his office and accessed the hard drive to see whether there was anything suspicious. He then claimed that when he found nothing suspicious, he returned the hard drive to us, but kept Shane's two computers.

None of this made any sense, and both Craig and Traci knew it was an outright lie. Even if one were to believe Khal, what he said he had done would be an obvious violation of internationally accepted protocol on the handling of evidence, making his actions worthy of further investigation. Rick and I left the

recount the details of our time in Singapore.

meeting feeling deflated, concerned, and confused. We began to wonder whose side our own government was on and whether they were really interested in uncovering the truth.

The next morning we met Ray Bonner in person for the first time. He was exactly what I had expected. His booming voice and expressive face fit his bigger-than-life personality perfectly. Our breakfast with Ray was fascinating and encouraging. He wanted to know every detail about our meeting with Craig and Traci, and was mesmerized by Craig's behavior towards us and the revelation of Khal's blatant lie. Recounting our stories to Ray was a pleasure because he listened as if his life depended on every detail. He took copious notes and his expressions were priceless. He would twist his face in the most unique way, his eyes would start to bulge, and he would exclaim, "This is great stuff!" Ray provided Rick and me with a sense of comfort and distraction, and we both grew to love him.

Later that afternoon, we met Traci for lunch at one of her favorite restaurants, a delicious little Indian food place. As we dined outside on plastic chairs, swatting flies, and fanning ourselves from the heat and humidity of the day, I could tell Traci was under a lot of stress and bothered about something. When I asked her what was going on, she told us that she had received news that one of her best friends had committed suicide that week. Throughout most of the lunch we talked about Traci's dear friend and the tremendous sadness she was experiencing. We could relate, and we felt very close to her as we cried together and shared our mutual pain. We also spoke briefly about Khal and his false claim about the hard drive. Traci encouraged us not to worry and said that he was probably trying to cover his tracks for shoddy police work.

The following day was an important one. We had meetings scheduled with the ambassador, Patrick Lo (Shane's boss at IME), and the Singapore police.

As Rick and I prepared for our meeting with Ambassador David Adelman, we encouraged each other not to get our hopes up. After the frosty reception we had received from Craig two days earlier, we were apprehensive and did not know what to expect. We were taken aback when we arrived at the embassy and Craig greeted us with a completely different disposition. He smiled and was polite as he informed us that he would be taking us to the ambassador's office and joining us in the meeting.

Craig escorted us to a large, distinguished reception area and introduced us to the ambassador's affable receptionist. After about 15 minutes of small talk, the ambassador came out of his office. He greeted us with a warm handshake and a welcoming look, apologizing for keeping us waiting. I immediately felt at ease, and my hopes were renewed as he graciously invited us into his office and told us to sit wherever we would like.

The office was stunning, reminiscent of one of the magnificent offices in the White House. Rick and I chose to sit on a couch, against the wall, facing the two high wing chairs where the ambassador and Craig sat. The contrast between Craig's initial demeanor towards us and the ambassador's was vast. With tears in his eyes, Ambassador Adelman expressed deep sympathy, telling us that he had four children of his own and that he could not imagine the pain that we were going through.

Throughout our hour and a half meeting, the ambassador listened intently, hanging on our every word. He was both compassionate and outraged by what we had been through. He told us that in his three years of being an ambassador, looking into Shane's death was his most important matter and highest priority. At the end of the meeting he thanked us profusely and said we had given him a lot to process. He also asked for the link to Shane's memorial service. Rick and I were impressed with the ambassador, and we left the embassy with a relieved sense that we had been listened to, that our country was finally behind us, and that this ambassador was going to take action.

Our meeting at IME was so unbelievable, it's almost hard to describe. We arrived by taxi and were met in the front lobby by a lawyer, a woman from human resources (HR), and a press agent. We were a little surprised by the entourage, but not nearly as surprised as we were when we reached our final destination: a large conference room with a huge table that could comfortably sit twenty-five people. Waiting for us were two police officers and Patrick Lo. Rick and I were seated on one side of the table by ourselves. On the other side sat the lawyer, the press agent, the HR representative, the two police officers, and Patrick Lo.

Patrick kept his head down throughout the whole meeting. He never once looked up at us. I was struck by how much Patrick's appearance had changed since we saw him last in June. He looked awful. His face was gray. His hair was gray. He appeared at least ten pounds heavier and twenty years older.

Rick began the meeting with a chuckle and said, "Wow, we didn't expect such a large welcoming committee. Thank you for coming." He then got serious and stated, "As you know, we believe our son was murdered, and that is why we are here." Rick then turned to Patrick Lo and said, "I'm not sure why you feel the need to include all these people. I only have a few simple questions."

The lawyer immediately interrupted Rick, saying, "You may address all your questions to me."

Rick first asked some innocuous questions in an attempt to put everyone at ease: "Shane received an award in the spring of this year? Do you remember the name of the award and when it was given? Was it associated with a monetary value? When was the last bonus Shane received awarded and when was it paid?"

The lawyer responded, "No comment."

Rick proceeded, "When did Shane first start meeting with Huawei representatives? When was his last meeting with them? Do you know the names of the attendees?"

The lawyer again said, "We cannot comment at this time."

"Very well," Rick continued, "Have the Singapore police contacted you about Huawei in relation to Shane? Have they interviewed you personally about Shane? Have they interviewed Dr. Kwong (IME's director)? Did they interview you about when the MOCVD or Veeco K4465I project began?"

Again there was no comment.

"Has the FBI contacted you about the transfer of sensitive technology to the Republic of China?"

The lawyer replied, "We have no information about this."

Rick proceeded, "An insider at IME told us that all employees had been forbidden to talk with outsiders about Shane. Did anybody at IME forbid the employees to talk about Shane with outsiders?"

Rick directed the question to Patrick, but the lawyer intercepted, "Patrick cannot comment," and then responded, "We cannot police these things. I don't know."

Rick concluded by asking if we could meet with some of Shane's friends. The lawyer said that would not be possible.

When Rick had finished, the IME lawyer emphatically declared, "This is the last meeting you are ever going to have with IME. Do not contact us ever again. Do not contact any of our employees. If you do, we will call the police. If there is any reason you need to communicate with IME, it must be done through the police." She continued, "Do you understand?"

Dumbfounded, we shook our heads affirming that we understood and then we were escorted out of the building, feeling like we were criminals.

The last item on our agenda was our meeting with the Singapore police. Craig accompanied us to the police station, where we were met by five top ranking police officers in a large, austere room. The meeting began with an apology that the highest-ranking officer could not be in attendance because he was on vacation. One of the officers then assured us that the police force was doing its very best to investigate the death of our son, and that they would go to any lengths to find the truth.

After Rick and I sat through what by this time we knew was a charade, I brought up Detective Khal's lie about the hard drive. No one contradicted me. No one said that Detective Khal was telling the truth. They simply sat with blank stares, reiterating that it was essential for their investigation that we hand over the hard drive. We made it clear that we would give them the hard drive if they would invite the FBI to assist with the investigation.

After our meeting with the officers, Detective Khal asked us to come back to the same interrogation room where we had first met immediately following Shane's death. Craig accompanied us. It felt creepy to be in that small, drab room again. Khal sat us down and handed me an inventory sheet of Shane's personal possessions that had been returned to us. He then asked, "Is this your signature?"

I replied, "Yes, this is my signature."

"Well done," Khal responded, "Right there is the proof that I gave you Shane's external hard drive. You signed for it."

The detailed inventory sheet included four of Shane's items that we had received.

1) one (1) laptop bag
2) one (1) wallet containing the following items:
    a. One (1) World USAA MasterCard
    b. One (1) adult EZ-link card
    c. One (1) USAA Cash rewards debit MasterCard
    d. One (1) SMRT Citibank Visa platinum
    e. One (1) Premier Miles Citibank Visa signature card
    f. One (1) Citibank ATM card
    g. One (1) California driver license
    h. One (1) name card
    i. One (1) 24 hour fitness USA card
    j. Cash amounting to $25/- (two pieces S$10-and one piece S$5/-)
3) Two (2) thumb drives
4) One (1) hard disk

Khal pointed to the last item on the inventory sheet and said, "See, there's the proof you signed for a hard disk."[8]

Rick, calling his bluff, said, "Okay, Khal. If you gave us that hard drive, can you describe what it looks like?"

Khal looked nervous and hesitated for a moment, then went on to describe a typical external hard drive: "black, flat, and rectangular, and I think it had two cords coming out of it."

Rick informed Khal that Shane's hard drive looks nothing like what he described. He then inquired, "This inventory sheet is so detailed. Why didn't you put the make, model, and serial number of the hard drive on it?"

Khal did not answer, so Rick continued, "Surely you have an evidentiary record of the make, model, and serial number of the hard drive, don't you?"

---

8   We believe that the hard disk on this list refers to a compact disc that was returned with Shane's things.

Khal responded that he wasn't sure if they did, but he would look into it.

In the meantime, Craig sat and witnessed this whole exchange. He knew Detective Khal never gave us that hard drive. He knew Khal couldn't even describe it to us. He knew that the police department didn't have the make, model, or serial number of it. He knew Khal had told a blatant lie, yet neither at that time nor later did he step in to speak on our behalf or question the inept handling of evidence by the police department or their duplicity.

Chapter 10

DEATH IN SINGAPORE

n spite of IME's hostility and Detective Khal's dishonesty, Rick and I felt our time in Singapore had been productive. We had accomplished what we set out to do—to meet with people and present our case. Returning home we faced the dreaded reality of Christmas without Shane. As the day drew near, I struggled not to be bitter, but to be grateful for the wonderful sons, husband, and life God had given me. I knew this is what Shane would want. But I felt like one of my limbs had been cut off, and I didn't know how I was going to function without it.

I wasn't the only one who didn't look forward to Christmas. The whole family just wanted it to slip by. Yet in the midst of incredible sorrow, we had a delightful day together. Our friends Andy and Tina Kasanicky joined us as we spent Christmas in loving tribute to Shane. We felt as if Shane were celebrating right along with us. He was mentioned in every conversation. We felt him in our tears and laughter. And every gift reflected something about him. One of the most touching and cherished gifts was from Andy, who had been the boys' youth leader in Florida. He gave each of them a set of two military style dog tags on a chain. One tag had an etched picture of all four boys and the quote, "There's no other love like the love of a brother, except the love from a brother." The other tag read:

Shane T. Todd
Loving Brother
1980-2012

Overall, our Christmas celebration provided an uplifting and hopeful ending to the most difficult and life-changing year of our lives.

Once we got over the awful hurdle of our first Christmas without Shane, Rick and I returned full-time to our mission of uncovering the truth. Meanwhile, the Singapore police continued their mission of persuading us to send them Shane's external hard drive. Even though we only had the Seagate external hard drive that we found in Shane's apartment, the police began to ask for two different "hard disks" (the one that Khal claimed he gave us and the one that we had found, which at one time the police had said were one and the same). Now, they requested that we send these two "hard discs," Shane's EZ link metro card, and Ashraf Massoud's forensic report.

After replying to the police that we would be able to comply with only part of their request, I emailed U.S. Consul Craig Bryant at the embassy and informed him that we had sent Ashraf's report, but that we did not have Shane's EZ link metro card. (I must have shredded it with Shane's credit cards, not thinking it would be important.) I also emphasized that we would send the one external hard drive that we had found in the apartment as soon as the police invited the FBI to join in the investigation.

Craig responded by urging us to comply to the police request without stipulation.

[February 3, 2013]

Mary:

Thanks for letting me know.

Just to be clear—the FBI is not involved, in any way, in the investigation of your son's death. It is very unlikely that the Singapore police will invite the FBI to become involved in the case at this stage, with the coroner's inquiry due to take place in one month.

It is your decision as to whether to turn the hard drive over to the police for examination. The police are asking for the hard drive because they believe that it contains information that is relevant to their investigation. Of course, if they don't have the opportunity to examine it, they won't be able to include any information from the hard drive in their report to the coroner. I would caution you that the coroner may then ask you and your husband, at the inquiry, why you withheld evidence from the police...

By this point, I was extremely frustrated that Craig did not understand or share our concerns about simply handing over the external hard drive to police officers who had already proved to be inept and dishonest. So I replied:

Dear Craig,

I'm not sure where you are coming from. The police have both of Shane's computers, his telephone, and his diary, so they are asking us for information that they already have. We believe the police have not displayed trustworthy behavior, which is why we are not willing to give them Shane's external hard drive without the FBI's involvement. The ambassador told us that the embassy is here to serve US citizens. It appears to us that you are more concerned with the Singapore police. Please forward this to the ambassador.

Mary Todd

Craig, however, ignored my rebuke and continued to do the bidding of the SPF:

Dear Rick and Mary:

Officer Sukhdev Singh of the Singapore police contacted me earlier this week. They are requesting that you provide the following items, which are pertinent to their investigation of Shane's death:

a. The hard disk which was handed over (by IO Khaldun) to you when you came here last June. The police need the disk to conduct a forensic examination.

b. The hard disk that you said you found in Shane's apartment (not the hard disk that IO Khaldun handed over to you). The police would also like to conduct an examination of this disk.

c. The EZ-link card which the police handed over to you last June. They can use the card to trace Shane's travels in the period before his death.

The police are also requesting a signed Privacy Act Waiver (PAW), which will allow the police to share information with the embassy.

The police may have already been in contact with you about this request; I know that these items were discussed when we met with the police in December. Please let me know, as soon as you can, whether you are going to send these items to the police. If you want to send them to me, I will be glad to deliver them to the police on your behalf. While it's your decision to make, I would urge you to comply with the request. <u>From what I've seen, I believe the police want to conduct a full and fair investigation, and providing these items will help to achieve that objective</u> [emphasis added]. But however you decide, please let me (or Officer Singh) know…

I was flabbergasted. After the lies the SPF had perpetrated from day one, how could Craig say that "the police want to conduct a full and fair investigation"?

Nevertheless, Craig continued to imply that Rick and I were the ones hindering the case and that we were the real the problem. He wrote:

> With regard to the items the police have requested you send to them—I think it's very important that you comply with their requests, and send what they have asked for. Your failure to do so could be viewed as an attempt to hinder the investigation... The FBI has no jurisdiction in Singapore, and cannot get involved in a case unless the government of Singapore specifically asks for assistance. To this point, the government has not asked for any assistance from the FBI, and I do not expect them to ask for assistance...

On February 14, we finally succumbed to Craig's incessant emails and asked Ashraf Massoud to send him a forensic copy of Shane's external Seagate hard drive. Rick also sent explicit instructions not to give the hard drive to the SPF, unless they agreed to give the FBI access to Shane's two computers.

On February 20, Craig informed us that he had received the copy of the hard drive and would deliver it to the police. Rick wrote back, reiterating, "Please ask for encased copies of Shane's computers. This is very important. There is no reason they should not be giving them to us. We need to know who accessed his hard drive!"

By this time, we should not have been surprised by Craig's response—but we were.

> Rick:
>
> I have not yet delivered the copy of the hard drive that you sent me to the police. Please acknowledge that I have your permission to do so.
>
> I will ask the police to send you [e]ncase[d] copies of Shane's computer, but I don't know what their response will be. They may simply refuse. But I don't want to be in the position of negotiating a deal between you and the police. That's not my role [emphasis added]. I think you should provide this copy to the police, because they have

requested it. But if you don't want to do that, let me know and I will return the copy to you, or put it in our safe.

Craig

I wanted to scream at the top of my lungs, "Excuse me! If it is not your role as the American consul to negotiate between the police and an American family, what exactly is your role?"

Thankfully, Rick calmly replied, "Craig, please just put the hard drive in the safe. I will make it clear to the police why it is important that we collaborate. You will not have to negotiate."

Craig once again responded that he did not "want to be put in the middle between the family and the police," and that he would return the hard drive by Federal Express. This made no sense to us, as he had already been advocating on behalf of the police.

Exasperated, Rick wrote a final response:

Craig,

I wish, with all my heart that we could trust the police. However, as you know, they are now claiming in the press, that they indeed gave us Shane's "hard disk drive." As you know, this is categorically untrue, which further deepens our mistrust of their integrity in the investigation of our son's death. For this reason, we cannot send them the hard drive **without outside oversight**. I would prefer that you keep the hard drive evidence in hopes that the police will partner with the FBI. However, if you will not do this, you may send us the hard drive. If this is your decision, do not inform the police until the hard drive is out of the country. Please forward this to the ambassador.

In the end, Craig refused to help us and returned the copy of the external hard drive.

While Rick and I were battling with Craig and the SPF over Shane's external hard drive, Ray Bonner, the journalist, was working tirelessly with Christine Spolar, Investigative Editor at the *Financial Times* (FT), to complete an article about Shane. The wait for its release was long and excruciating. Ray kept announcing a publication date, only to postpone it time and time again. He always apologized for the delays and made it clear that he was just as disappointed as we were. He explained that in order to avoid a lawsuit, the FT lawyers were working over-time to ensure that every detail was accurate.

Finally, on February 16, 2013 after five weeks of delays, the day we so eagerly anticipated arrived! On the front cover of the FT weekly magazine, in bold black and white letters, the headline read, "Death in Singapore." Under it was the caption, "A young American electronics engineer is found hanged. He had feared his work was compromising US security. What really happened to Shane Todd?" The article included an eight-page spread with colored pictures of Shane, the family, and the hard drive, along with a description of Shane's life and the mystery surrounding his death.

Perhaps the most important and intriguing part of the article was the explanation of Shane's work at IME and what information on his hard drive revealed about a collaborative project between IME and the Chinese company Huawei regarding highly specialized gallium nitride (GaN) technology. As an FT article link explains, GaN is an advanced semiconductor material that can handle far higher temperatures and far more data than silicone. It is used commercially to enhance the capabilities of high-end electronics such as cellphones and blue ray disc players, but it also has significant military applications, particularly in the realm of radar and surveillance systems. In fact, concern over this latter application, has led the U.S. government to impose export controls on equipment used in the production of GaN.

The article reported that shortly after joining IME in December 2010, Shane was appointed the leader of a five-man team focused on GaN devices. According to documents found on his hard drive, Shane then "began to work on what was apparently a joint project between IME and Huawei to develop a GaN amplifier," and in September 2011 created a folder labeled "Huawei." According to the FT report, this folder included "a file entitled 'Schedule 1 Huawei GaN

Spec 01,' and this contained a 'Project Plan' that outlined objectives, scope and a timetable for the proposed collaboration between IME and Huawei." Around that same time, Shane was instructed by IME to find "equipment pivotal to GaN research."

Shane determined that a New York Company, Veeco, manufactured the necessary equipment. IME then purchased a custom made MOCVD machine from Veeco and wrote up a "proposal" in November 2011, which included instructions for Shane's training with engineers at the Veeco facility in New Jersey. The "proposal" noted that Veeco stated "that they will not directly transfer the best known method recipes to our tool, rather we [IME] will copy the recipe first hand during our visit." Also found in another of Shane's files was a statement concerning the GaN recipe: "Can share during training but not available for technology transfer."

Because the equipment IME purchased from Veeco was considered "dual use," meaning it could be used in both commercial and military applications, it required an export license from the U.S. Commerce Department. Although Veeco would not release a copy of the license, Shane's hard drive contained a file entitled "Export License—IME—Completed." Included in that file were statements from IME defining the nature of their research as "commercial applications," and declaring that the "end use" of the equipment "will be developing recipes for growing [gallium nitride on silicon] for power electronic devices that support industrial partners in Singapore."

In spite of this statement that the technology would be used for electronic devices in Singapore, the FT report explains that the connection between Huawei, IME and Veeco implied by these documents "would be problematic for Veeco and IME because Huawei has been deemed a security risk by powerful US lawmakers." In response to questions from FT about such collaboration, both IME and Huawei denied having any such business relationship. Scott Sykes, Huawei's head of international media, declared, "We are not aware of any of this;" and, "We have not had any co-operation with IME with respect to GaN so there is nothing more to add."

Following publication of the FT article, however, both Huawei and IME changed their story and admitted that they had engaged in preliminary talks about a commercial project, but stated that nothing ever came of them.[9] Huawei spokesman Scott Sykes sent a statement to FT contending, "IME approached Huawei on one occasion to co-operate with them in the GaN field, but we decided not to accept, and consequently do not have any co-operation related to GaN." Similarly, IME's director, Dr. Dim-Lee Kwong, sent a letter to FT stating, "Neither IME nor Shane was involved in any classified research project. The institute did not go beyond preliminary talks with Huawei on a commercial project and does not have, and has never had, a project with the company on GaN amplifiers."[10]

Although Huawei and IME claimed that they only engaged in preliminary talks about a project of a commercial nature that did not involve GaN amplifiers, Shane's hard drive revealed a different story. In fact, in preparation for publication of "Death in Singapore," the FT engaged two experts in GaN technology to review the "Huawei" project file from Shane's hard drive. The first expert, Professor Sir Colin Humphreys, the director of research at the Cambridge University Centre for Gallium Nitride, said that the project "was a plan for a GaN-based high-electron mobility transistor—and amplifier with commercial and military applications." He further stated, "You can't say it is 100 percent for military use. There are many civilian uses. [But] you would be foolish not to think of military uses because there is a huge market for it." Sir Colin also told FT that the phrasing suggesting that Veeco might be willing to share a technology recipe was unusual: "Normally you'd expect the recipe to be put on the machine. What the proposal says is: they won't put it on the equipment but they will make it available."

The second expert, Steven Huettner, had worked in the missile defense industry for more than 30 years. Huettner called the Huawei project plan "disturbing." And, although he acknowledged that the "project could be aimed at producing high power transmitters for mobile phone towers," he contended that the specifications of the project "jump out at you." Huettner concluded by

---

9   Feng Zengkun, "Huawei Denies Work with IME in Researcher's Field," *Straits Times*, February 19, 2013.

10   Christine Spolar and Raymond Bonner, "Huawei Says Singapore Agency Project Was Not Pursued," *Financial Times*, February 22, 2013.

stating that the project "absolutely has military potential," and that "an obvious use would be for high-powered radar that could enhance... military capability."

Following publication of "Death in Singapore," the SPF immediately went into damage control and released the following statement on February 17 defending their investigation into the death of Shane Todd:

The police investigate all unnatural death cases thoroughly, working closely with the pathologist and other relevant experts, and no prior assumptions are made on the cause of death. Our procedures for investigating cases, particularly those involving death of persons, are strict and of high international standards. We have handled this case in the same way as other cases that the police have looked into.

All crime scene locations which have the potential for recovery of evidence are handled with care and are protected from interference of any kind so as to preserve any trace of evidence. The sites are secured by police for the duration required for the scene examination and evidence collection. The conditions and items found at the crime scene are carefully recorded in great detail, as well as conserved and removed for subsequent laboratory analysis.

The Financial Times article mentioned a hard disk which was purportedly recovered by Mr. and Mrs. Rick Todd from their son's residence. To ensure the investigations are as thorough as possible, we urge any person who has evidence in their possession that can assist in our investigation to share them with the police.

All relevant evidence gathered by police will be tendered at the coroner's inquiry once the investigations are complete. The coroner will independently determine the circumstances under which Mr. Shane Todd came by his death taking into account the investigation findings and other evidence. During the open inquiry, the family of the deceased may question the witnesses and the relevant reports, including the pathologist report. As investigations are ongoing, it is inappropriate for the police to comment further on the case.

Since the death of Mr. Shane Todd, the police have engaged and assisted the family without impeding the objectivity of our investigation process. We will continue to do so. Police have also kept the American Embassy and the FBI informed of the case.[11]

I couldn't believe the SPF's deceitful statement. If the police had made "no prior assumptions on the cause of death," why were we initially given a completely inaccurate account of how Shane allegedly hanged himself? Furthermore, the SPF claims that their investigation procedures "are strict and of high international standards" and that they carefully "preserve any trace of evidence" were ludicrous. The police clearly mishandled evidence in many instances. The following are just a few of the most egregious examples:

- Detective Khal, the investigating officer, accessed one of Shane's computers at the scene claiming that's how he found the suicide notes.
- Khal had Shane's computers in his possession for six weeks before turning them over to forensics to be secured and analyzed.
- According to phone records, Shane's phone was used after his death.
- The scene of death was not secured—the apartment was left unlocked, and there was no crime tape or dusting for fingerprints.

Also, if—as claimed in their statement—the police carefully record items found at the crime scene and remove them for subsequent laboratory analysis, why did they never mention the Seagate external hard drive in their detailed records? And why would Khal have given it back to us, as he claimed he did, before it had been analyzed?

Along with their efforts to save face, the SPF's desperation to gain possession of Shane's hard drive grew. On February 27, Tan Chee Kiong, the SPF head investigator, wrote a certified letter to Cary Gleicher, the FBI legal attaché in Singapore. Kiong did not solicit FBI help with the investigation, rather he asked for help in convincing us to hand over the hard drive. Kiong wrote, "In the course of the investigation, the deceased's parents had informed us that they

---

11   Christine Spolar, "Police Defend Probe Into Singapore Death," *Financial Times*, February 17, 2013.

found an external hard disk in his apartment which may contain information relevant to our investigation. Arising from this, we subsequently requested the deceased's parents to hand over the said hard disk to us for the purpose of investigation, but they did not accede to our request." Kiong concluded by asking Gleicher to "speak to the deceased's parents and convince them to hand over the said hard-disk."

The publication of the FT article changed everything. After months of begging for someone to listen to us, we now had the world's attention. The day after the article was released, Rick and I flew to Southern California to stay at my mother's house, where our cell phones rang incessantly with calls from the media, investigative reporters, and movie producers. We were interviewed on a number of radio stations and several major news networks filmed Rick and me, in my mother's living room, telling our story. During this time, we also met with Ryan Smith and Paul La Rosa from CBS's documentary/news magazine show "48 Hours." We were so impressed by Ryan and Paul's professionalism and sincere interest in Shane's case that we agreed to an exclusive deal allowing them to document our story.[12]

All of this attention was surreal, and frankly, it would have been exciting had it not been about the death of our son. In reality, it was a constant and painful reminder of our horrendous situation. At the same time, however, it gave us hope: We were finally getting the opportunity to tell the world our story, which might get us closer to the truth about what happened to our son.

There is no doubt that if it were not for Ray Bonner and the *Financial Times'* article, "Death in Singapore," we would never have received this kind of attention, and Christina and I would not be writing this book. We would simply be, like so many other families who have lost a child overseas under suspicious circumstances, frustrated and alone, seeking help—but to no avail.

---

12   "48 Hours" later produced an award winning documentary on Shane's case entitled, "Lies, Spies, & Secrets," which originally aired on October 5, 2013. The link to the episode can be found at www.justice4shanetodd.com.

Chapter 11

A LAW FIRM ON EVERY CORNER

hortly after the *Financial Times* (FT) published "Death in Singapore," Rick and I received a phone call from Virginia Congressman Frank Wolf, inviting us to Washington D.C. to meet with him and several high-ranking FBI officials. We recognized that this invitation was a huge step forward for our case. Congressman Wolf serves on the powerful House Appropriations Committee and is the chairman of the Commerce-Justice-Science Subcommittee that funds the Commerce Department and the Justice Department (which includes the FBI).

Additionally, Congressman Wolf had a special interest in our case. In 2006, his office computers were targeted in a cyber-attack by Chinese operatives that resulted in the theft of valuable information. Since that time, Congressman Wolf has worked diligently to protect our country from cyber espionage and has been instrumental in funding efforts to combat cyber-attacks from state-owned or government associated Chinese telecom equipment manufacturers, such as Huawei.

The timing of Wolf's call couldn't have been better as "48 Hours" producer Ryan Smith was currently in Montana filming us. Ryan asked if he could accompany us to Washington, and when we enthusiastically agreed, he arranged for an entire film crew to meet us there. In the meantime, Rick and I were able to contact and make appointments with our two Montana senators, Max Baucus and Jon Tester, and our state representative, Steve Daines. We invited our boys to join us, but John was the only one who could clear his schedule; Chet was running the family bed and breakfast, and Dylan was attending classes at the University of Montana.

On Thursday, February 28, 2013, our first morning in Washington, the "48 Hours" crew met Rick and me in front of our hotel with two black SUVs. We piled into the first SUV with the producer Ryan Smith, the correspondent Peter Van Sant, and two camera men. The rest of the crew followed. As we drove to the Capitol Building, Van Sant asked us a series of questions such as: "What are you feeling now that your story is finally gaining national recognition?" "What do you hope to accomplish today?" "What has brought you to this point?" As we answered the questions, we were constantly reminded to "look natural," "look out the window," "point your finger at that building," and "talk to each other." The whole experience was surreal—it was hard to "act natural" when we knew that we were being recorded for broadcast to a national audience.

Our first meeting of the day was with Senator Jon Tester and his chief of staff, Tom Lopach. Senator Tester was the quintessential Montana cowboy, self-assured and sturdy looking, sporting cowboy boots. Upon our arrival, Tester proudly showed off his office, which was filled with pictures of his Montana ranch. We spent about half-an-hour with the senator, who opened the meeting by talking at length about his love for Montana. When we were given the opportunity to share, Tester listened, but his chief of staff was the one who took notes and asked questions. The senator ended the meeting by assuring us that he would see what he could do. Although the meeting was pleasant, it did not engender great confidence that it would achieve any results.

Our next meeting was with Congressman Daines, who was newly elected to office. He looked stunned, as we told him about the death of our son. It was obvious he did not know much about the background related to our situation and why we were seeking an audience with him and had no clue as to what he should do in response. Our only firm conclusion from that meeting was that Daines was so new to Congress, that he did not, at that time, know how to help us.

After a fairly unproductive day, we headed to the hotel restaurant to unwind and enjoy dinner with the "48 Hours" crew. Our son John flew in that evening and joined us for dinner. My heart weld up with pride when he came strolling across the dining room, dressed in his pilot uniform, smiling engagingly. We sat in the restaurant for hours, enjoying one another's company and discussing the important day ahead.

The next morning, we awoke to the FT headline "Senator Takes Todd Death to White House."[13] The article, written by FT reporter Richard McGregor and correspondent Ray Bonner, announced that "Max Baucus, a Democratic Montana senator, and Frank Wolf, a Republican member of the House of Representatives from Virginia, are both due to meet the Todd family in Washington." The article also stated that Senator Baucus had discussed the case with the White House and several Singaporean officials and quoted him saying, "As a father my heart is broken for Shane's parents and I will do everything in my power to help them get the answers they deserve." Our day was certainly starting off on a promising note!

With the "48 Hours" crew still filming our every move, Rick, John, and I headed to our first meeting with Congressman Wolf. We were met by Wolf's legislative director, Thomas Culligan, who ushered us into an impressive office and introduced us to the congressman, a distinguished looking gentleman, with a full head of white hair. I was immediately encouraged by Wolf's serious demeanor, which seemed appropriate considering the matter we had come to

13   Richard McGregor and Raymond Bonner, "Senator Takes Todd Death to White House," *Financial Times*, February 28, 2013.

discuss. Wolf informed us that we would first hold a private meeting and then representatives from the FBI would join us.

As Rick and I prepared to present the evidence we had compiled, we were taken aback, but pleased, when Congressman Wolf informed us that he was already familiar with our story and that he believed us. He emphasized that what he really wanted to know was how he could be of help to us.

We responded to Wolf's generous gesture by telling him that we were seeking a congressional investigation into the death of our son. Wolf looked at us intently and grimly responded, "You are doing the right thing to press for a congressional investigation, but you are not going to get anywhere."

Shocked and bewildered, I asked, "Why not?"

I will never forget Wolf's blunt reply: "Huawei has a law firm on every corner in Washington D.C. and has helped elect several current members of Congress."

Even though I heard Wolf's words, I could not believe what he was claiming: *"Does China really have that much influence over our country's political decisions?"* At that moment, I realized that Congressman Wolf was warning us that our quest for truth would be a battle, not only against Singapore, but also against the ubiquitous influence of China and its sway over members of our own government.

Shortly after Wolf's disturbing revelation, he ushered in a group of FBI agents and introduced each one by name and position. The agents had all been briefed on Shane's story, and they assured us that they would do what they could to investigate his death. They did caution, however, that we probably would not hear much from them about the case because they would need to keep information confidential during the open investigation. One agent said, "In fact, you may never hear or know what the FBI is doing in your son's case."

Our final order of business was to hand over Shane's external Seagate hard drive to the FBI for analysis. We signed the papers documenting the handover procedure and included explicit instructions that the FBI not share the hard drive with the SPF unless they were invited to fully engage in the investigation.

Following our meeting with Congressman Wolf and the FBI, a staff member from Senator Baucus' office met us and accompanied us to the Capitol Building for a conference with ABC News. She then introduced us to Laura Rauch, Military Legislative Assistant to Senator Baucus, and a few other staff members. Baucus' staff kindly invited us to join them for lunch before an interview with Megyn Kelly from Fox News and our afternoon meeting with Senator Baucus.

Senator Baucus greeted us in his folksy, ranch-style reception room with a compassionate smile and warm handshake. After a few moments of small talk and a quick interview with "48 Hours," Baucus led us to a conference room, where we were joined by his executive assistant, his chief of finance, his press agent, and Laura Rauch. They all knew about Shane's death and offered sincere condolences.

Senator Baucus told us to call him "Max," and after beckoning everyone to take a seat, explained that he had read the FT article and was horrified over what had happened. He announced, "I smell something rotten in this whole affair, and I will do everything in my power to get to the bottom of this." He then encouraged us to tell the full story from our perspective, to which he listened intently.

After we related our saga, Baucus asked what he could do to help. We told him that we were seeking a congressional investigation and that we had prepared a list of documents we wanted from the FBI:

- A copy of the International in Arms Regulations (ITAR) document that Shane would have signed with Veeco before training on the MOCVD machine
- A report detailing how much access the FBI was given by the SPF to Shane's two computers, cell phone, and diary, and the bureau's findings on such
- A report detailing which operating system was connected to Shane's external Seagate hard drive after his death

We also asked Senator Baucus to solicit from the FBI an independent pathology report, and a forensic analysis of Shane's writing style in comparison to the alleged suicide notes. Baucus agreed to co-author a letter with Senator Tester to the FBI requesting that they respond to us.

Baucus ended the meeting by giving us his personal contact information and encouraging us to call him directly if there were anything more he could do. He also invited us to return to Washington D.C. the following week to meet with Singapore's Minister for Foreign Affairs and Minister for Law, K. Shanmugam. Referring to Minister Shanmugam, Baucus stated, "I want him to see the face of the parents whose son was killed in his country."

Rick and I were encouraged by the meeting and touched when the senator personally escorted us down the halls of the Capitol and through the Hart Building to the underground train station to bid us farewell.

A couple days later, Rick and I returned to Washington D.C. to meet with Minister Shanmugam. Throughout the entire meeting, Shanmugam assured us that the SPF was one of the finest police forces in the world and that they were working hard to thoroughly investigate the death of our son. He promised that Singapore would carry out an open and transparent investigation and would share any relevant evidence with the FBI, but he was totally disinterested in discussing or viewing the evidence we had compiled. Shanmugam was clearly more concerned with pacifying us than with acquiring the truth.

A week and a half after we returned to Montana, we discovered through various media sources that Minister Shanmugam was still in Washington D.C. and was scheduled to meet with Senator Baucus, Secretary of State John Kerry, Attorney General Eric Holder, and various other government officials, including Arizona Senator John McCain.

Prior to these meetings, *USA Today* cited Senator Baucus, emphasizing that the SPF and Singaporean government "have been less than forthcoming" in the Shane Todd case and that evidence he had seen so far raised "very, very strong questions" and "deep concerns about national security."[14]

In a press conference, directly following his March 12 meeting with Senator Baucus, Minister Shanmugam emphatically claimed that IME had not engaged in any unauthorized or illegal technology transfers and that the company was subject to rigorous government audits. Shanmugam also pledged that the SPF

---

14 Oren Dorrell, "Senator, Parents Press Singapore in Son's Death," *USA Today*, March 12, 2013.

would share the evidence in their possession with the FBI and highlighted that "a public and fully transparent Corner's Inquiry will be held in which the Todd family could participate and pose questions."[15]

Later that same day, Senator Baucus called me personally to report on his meeting with Minister Shanmugam. Baucus told me that, during the meeting, Shanmugam claimed that IO Khal had never given us that initial false description of how Shane allegedly hanged himself. Shanmugam also stated that two U.S. pathologists had concluded that Shane's death was a typical case of suicide by hanging. Baucus asked me to send him a timeline of the events that led up to Shane's death and what had transpired since then. I responded with the following email:

> Dear Senator Baucus,
>
> Thank you for your call today. It is disconcerting, yet not surprising, that the Foreign Affairs Minister to Singapore lied about the SPF description of how Shane hanged himself, and about the two separate U.S. pathologist reports. Attached is one of the many timelines that I sent to the U.S. Embassy in Singapore, and the pathologist report.
>
> You will never know, this side of heaven, how much your help means to us and to our country.
>
> Thank you,
> Mary Todd

Senator Baucus replied with a simple, "Thanks, Mary. This helps a lot. We'll get to the bottom of this. Many more leads to pursue."

A couple days later, *USA Today* reported that Senators Baucus and Tester had introduced an amendment to a Senate budget resolution that would withhold a $500,000 Department of Defense research grant to Shane's former employer, IME, until the SPF gave the FBI full access to evidence relevant to Shane Todd's

---

15   Singapore Ministry of Foreign Affairs Press Statement: "Visit by Minister for Foreign Affairs and Minister for Law K Shanmugam to the United States of America: Meetings with US Secretary of State John Kerry and Attorney-General Eric Holder and Other Personalities, 12 to 13 March 2013."

death.[16] Senator Baucus reported, "Singapore's promise to share all evidence with the FBI is a significant step forward, and I appreciate the minister's time and attention to Shane's case. Now we have to keep the pressure on to ensure that commitment is fulfilled." Senator Tester additionally stated that the amendment "is a way to hold Singapore accountable and let them know we're serious [about getting answers for the Todd family]."

In response to this measure, a spokesman for Singapore's Ministry of Foreign Affairs (MFA) issued a press release stating:

> We are deeply disappointed by the Senators' actions and statements. The Senators had requested the FBI to be given "full access" to all the evidence in the investigation conducted by the Singapore Police Force (SPF) over the case, based on the version of the facts provided by the family alone. The SPF so far has refrained from publicizing the information they have gathered because investigations are ongoing, after which there will be a public Coroner's Inquiry where all the facts will be laid out to determine the cause of Mr Todd's death...
>
> The issue of applying "pressure" should not arise between countries, which have had a long, open and cooperative relationship with each other based on mutual respect. Singapore has made every effort to be open and transparent in both the investigation of Mr Todd's death and the IME's projects. We will let the outcome of the investigation and Coroner's Inquiry speak for themselves.[17]

Following this high profile week, investigative reporter Ray Bonner observed, "Well, you certainly have the world's attention now." And, for the remainder of March, we continued to attract significant media interest. We were interviewed on either radio or television almost every day, and several film crews flew to

---

16 Oren Dorell, "Senators: Block Singapore Funds for Shane Todd Evidence," *USA Today*, March 14, 2013.

17 Singapore Ministry of Foreign Affairs Press Statement: "MFA Spokesman's Comments in Response to Media Queries on US Senators' Introduction of an Amendment to Block US Funding the Institute of Microelectronics," March 17, 2013.

Montana to document our story, including Miguel Marquez from CNN's "Erin Burnett Out Front."

In the midst of all the media attention, we also experienced some disturbing computer problems. Around mid-March, I noticed strange occurrences on my computer. By coincidence, I discovered that every email I sent had an attachment of Shane's psychological evaluation from the doctor in Singapore. I could not remove the attachment, so I called a local FBI agent, Steve Liss, and asked him what I should do. That evening, Steve came to our apartment with a computer specialist. After examining my computer, the specialist confirmed it had been hacked. Since that time, my computer and cell phone have continued to operate in a peculiar manner—for example: when I answer my phone there is often a delayed response, sometimes I don't receive voicemail messages for a couple of days, and I frequently do not receive emails related to the case until hours after they are sent—which makes me wonder if my email and conversations are being monitored.

Another curious move was that the Coroner's Inquiry was changed from two days in March to eleven days in May. In mid-January, IO Khal had emailed us stating that "the Coroner's Inquiry has been fixed on 4th & 5th March 2013 (tentative) commencing at 9.30 am daily." Shortly after publication of the FT article, however, we received an email from Craig Bryant, U.S. Consul in Singapore, informing us that the inquiry had been rescheduled to May 13-27. In this email, Craig encouraged us to hire a lawyer to represent our case in court. I remember feeling bewildered: "If the Coroner's Inquiry is supposed to be a transparent fact-finding inquiry into the death of our son, with the goal of all concerned parties to uncover the truth, why on earth would we need a lawyer?"

Chapter 12

THE PRO BONO LAWYER

btaining legal representation became our first priority as we prepared for the Coroner's Inquiry. Since the inquest was supposed to be a fact-finding analysis of how Shane died—not a criminal trial—we hadn't understood why we couldn't just present the evidence ourselves. Yet, after U.S. Consul Craig Bryant, the SPF, Ray Bonner, and others emphatically told us to hire a lawyer, we decided to take their advice. The American Embassy sent us a list of recommended attorneys, and friends and a family member recommended others, but we soon discovered that finding a lawyer in Singapore willing to take our case was no easy task. Not one of the lawyers recommended by the embassy would agree to represent us. Several firms responded to Rick's queries by stating that our case was too volatile and the political ramifications were too serious for them to get involved. One U.S. law firm, with a branch office in Singapore, said they would only take on the case if the inquest were held in the United States; they wouldn't go near it in Singapore.

Once Rick exhausted the list of recommended lawyers with no luck, he began to search online for criminal lawyers. Finally, Rick received a positive response from Zhengxi Choo (Remy), who said he had read about Shane's death in the *Financial Times* and was willing to take on our "high-profile" case. The same day that Rick and I planned to sign a retainer agreement with Remy, Rick heard back from another lawyer, Gloria James-Civetta, whom he had contacted weeks earlier through Facebook. Gloria informed Rick that she was on the board of the Singapore Law Society's Pro Bono Committee and that she and her team members would be pleased to assist with our case.

Since our trip to Singapore was already going to be a huge financial burden, the phrase "pro bono" caught Rick's attention. When he emailed Gloria to ask about her legal fees, she responded, "Basically, no professional fees charged except to cover [the] law firm's disbursements. Further, you have the benefit of a team of lawyers selected by me, as I also sit as the vice-chairman of the criminal law practice committee of the law society of Singapore."

Before signing any paperwork, Rick specifically asked Gloria whether she was willing and capable to take on the Singapore government (including the SPF or any other state agency) and whether she was tied in any way to the state, Huawei, or IME.

Gloria replied, "We are not conflicted, nor are we afraid to take on authorities."

We later realized that we should have paid closer attention to this wording, in which Gloria avoided directly answering the question of whether or not she had ties to the state, Huawei, or IME. Nevertheless, Rick and I wanted to believe that Gloria was truly seeking to help us, so we accepted her statement at face value.

After Ray Bonner looked into Gloria's legal background and found nothing amiss, we were confident that she could provide competent representation. We signed a contract with her on April 1, 2013, less than six weeks before the inquiry was scheduled to begin. The following day, Gloria presented her legal team: Steven Lam, a senior corporate lawyer from an international law firm; Foo Cheow Ming, a criminal litigation lawyer; and Amarjit Singh, a criminal lawyer. Shortly before the inquiry, Peter Ong Lip Cheng, a criminal lawyer with a background in murder investigation, also joined the team.

We began corresponding with Gloria via email everyday and we would Skype with the whole team once or twice a week. Rick and I were very grateful for this pro bono legal team, who—at the time—appeared eager to help us and make a name for themselves in our high profile case.

Filling Gloria in on all the evidence was an arduous process. There was so much information to go over. Additionally, we were continually uncovering more details that supported our case. On April 8, Rick emailed Gloria with information he had just received from an inside source at IME. According to this contact, Dr. Kwong (IME's director) had transferred Shane into IME's GaN research group—even though it was not Shane's primary area of expertise—because Shane was the only person on his staff who was a U.S. citizen. As a U.S. citizen, Shane could be trained on the Veeco MOCVD machine and get access to the training manuals. In order to gain such access, however, IME had to sign an International Traffic in Arms Regulations (ITAR) document.

ITAR governs the export and import of defense-related information, technology, and services and dictates that items covered by the regulations cannot be shared with non-U.S. citizens, unless a specific exemption is granted by the U.S. government. It is our understanding that under ITAR rules, Shane would not be able to give the Veeco training manuals to foreign users. When Shane returned from training at Veeco, he became very uncomfortable with the relationship IME had formed with Huawei, and the position that he was in. He believed that he could be compromising U.S. security and violating U.S. export law. We believe this is why he told us, "they are asking me to do things that I am uncomfortable doing," and "I think I might be betraying my country." Shortly after saying that, Shane decided to quit his job at IME, and repeatedly told us he felt his life was being threatened, never overtly, but in subtle, clear ways.

Gloria informed us that we would receive a package with evidence the police had compiled at least two weeks before the inquiry, as required by Singapore law. At that point, she said we could add any information we had to the body of evidence. We were anxious to receive this evidentiary package from the police, so we could finally determine whether they were even considering the possibility of homicide, but we waited and waited to no avail. Gloria related that the police kept promising to deliver it, but failed to follow through.

During this time, we also held weekly Skype conversations with Shirley, Shane's girlfriend. Shirley was extremely upset because the police repeatedly called her back to the station for interrogation. She told us that they were pressuring her to change her testimony and to say that she found Shane hanging by a strap, not a cord. Shirley was steadfast, however, and continued to tell them that when she found Shane he had a thin cord around his neck and that she did not remember seeing a towel. This was significant because the police insisted that they had found Shane with a towel and strap around his neck. On several occasions, Shirley called us crying because the police were so persistent. Wanting to help, we wrote the embassy asking for their advice and whether they could provide an advocate to accompany Shirley during her meetings with the police. The embassy representative told us that since Shirley was from the Philippines, there was nothing the U.S. Embassy could do for her, and that she should contact the Philippine Embassy. When Shirley did call her embassy, however, they were unwilling to assist her.

In addition to pressuring Shirley, the police also were in contact with Ashraf Massoud, the computer forensic expert who had analyzed Shane's external Seagate hard drive. The SPF told Ashraf that they would pay his way to Singapore and that they needed to go over his evidence and get his conditional statement. We were surprised and grateful that they were willing to pay for Ashraf to travel to Singapore so he could give his testimony; however, on this too, they never followed through. They kept promising to send Ashraf a travel date, with his hotel and ticket confirmation, but they never did. Several times the SPF gave Ashraf a tentative date, only to postpone it.

On May 3, less than two weeks before the inquiry, Ashraf emailed us, "I know the wheels of government turn slowly, but I've not heard anything yet. Can you follow up for me?"

Rick wrote Gloria asking if she could do something: "Ashraf has not received any info. He needs to plan his work schedule. Do you know what is up? Also, do you know what is happening on the prosecution side?"

Interestingly enough, Gloria did not respond to our question about Ashraf, but she did inform us that she had received word that the police would be handing over the evidentiary bundle the following morning and that she would go into the office to verify and receive it. But the following day came and went with no word from Gloria about the evidence.

As it was then only a week and a half before the inquiry, we realized that the SPF never intended to book Ashraf's ticket nor give us the police evidence or the conditional statements in the required time frame. Finally, we told Ashraf to go ahead and purchase his own ticket, and if the state didn't reimburse him, we would. To this day they have not done so, in spite of our repeated requests.

Once Ashraf had his ticket, the Singapore police called him and asked for his flight number. They wanted to pick him up at the airport and immediately get his conditional statement. They also said that they would provide a place for Ashraf to stay. Ashraf, who being in law enforcement wasn't as trusting as us, declined their invitation and told them he had already made arrangements. He also remained vague about his flight information, as he didn't want to give the SPF the opportunity to skew his testimony by making him provide a conditional statement in the middle of the night, directly following an eighteen-hour flight.

At this point, we should have accepted that the Coroner's Inquiry wasn't going to be a non-adversarial fact-finding pursuit, but we still had hope. It wasn't until we got to court that we realized fully how naive we were and the incredible amount of power and resources we were up against.

In the final days before our trip, the thought of returning to Singapore made me feel ill. Thankfully, several factors made the whole ordeal seem more bearable. For one, all three of our sons and our daughter-in-law Corynne, were able to clear their schedules so they could accompany us. And American Airlines, the company Rick works for, generously provided flights for the six of us. We were further comforted when my brother, Richard Elwell, and Rick's sister, Mary Williamson, made arrangements and paid their way to join us in Singapore. Our loved ones who could not physically go with us pledged to be with us in prayer and to contact us daily through emails or Skype. It was reassuring to know that, whatever we faced, we would not be alone.

On May 6, 2103, Rick and I were the first of our group to arrive in Singapore. We came a week before the inquiry to meet with our lawyers and familiarize ourselves with the evidence, but the SPF still had not delivered the evidentiary package as they had promised and was required by law.

Gloria and U.S. Consul Craig Bryant picked us up at the airport in an embassy van complete with a driver. We immediately began to discuss the inquiry, and I asked if Traci was still in Singapore, so she could testify. Craig shook his head no and said that she had already been transferred to her next post.

Stunned, I inquired, "Will she be able to give her testimony via Skype?"

Gloria informed us that neither Craig nor Traci would be able to testify due to diplomatic immunity.

I looked Craig in the eye and asked, "Is this true?"

Craig didn't say anything. He just nodded his head.

Rick and I were outraged. We didn't understand what diplomatic immunity had to do with our case, and both Craig and Traci's testimony were essential. Traci could testify that the police had read us a false narrative of how Shane allegedly hanged himself, and Craig could testify that the police did not have the description, make, model, or serial number of the external hard drive which Khal was fallaciously claiming he had given us. We begged Craig to provide testimony, but with a deadpan expression on his face, he replied that the matter was out of his hands.

In response to our distress, Gloria reassured us, "There's nothing to worry about. We're all on the same team. The state prosecution and your legal defense are all working toward the same goal of finding the truth." This same statement, which was proved to be categorically untrue, was repeated over and over by various parties just like the mantra, "there is no murder in Singapore."

Even though I had a hard time believing what Gloria said, her words did make me feel better and I started to relax. She continued to explain that the Coroner's Inquiry would be a non-adversarial examination of the evidence. She also told us that she knew the judge to be a fair man and was pleased with his selection.

Craig and Gloria dropped us off at the complex where we had arranged to stay. After making plans to meet with Gloria and the legal team the next day, we said goodbye. With heavy hearts, Rick and I hauled our luggage toward our third floor condo. As I trudged through the complex, I observed that it was beautifully landscaped and clean, but it felt cold and uninviting. I remember thinking, "What are we doing here? Is this really our life?" I felt like my senses were in overload—I was aware of every breath and every heartbeat, and I felt completely overwhelmed.

The following day, I wrote my first email to friends and family. I told them that, in spite of our dreadful circumstances and the growing fear of what we would face during the inquiry, my morning Bible reading had calmed and encouraged me. The reading from my daily devotional included the Old Testament account of David and Goliath and the following selection from Psalm 57:

> Enemies, like lions, are all around me; I must lie down among them. Their teeth are like spears and arrows, their tongues as sharp as swords. God is supreme over the skies; his Majesty covers the earth. They set a trap for me. I am very worried. They dug a pit in my path, but they fell into it themselves. My heart is steady, God; my heart is steady....

I felt as if God were preparing my heart for a David and Goliath-like battle. Though we didn't have the power of state authority, financial backing, or the best attorneys—we did have one potent rock in our sling: an unwavering determination to uncover the truth.

***

Although we had already been informed that U.S. Vice-Consul Traci Goins and U.S. Consul Craig Bryant were claiming diplomatic immunity and would not testify, we wanted a written record that we had requested their testimony, so on May 8, we sent Gloria the following list of requested witnesses:

- **Ashraf Massoud**: forensic computer analyst
- **Dylan Todd**: brother

- **John Todd**: brother
- **Steve Huettner**: Chief Engineer at Nuvotronics, expert in GaN applications and uses
- **Singh Sukhdev**: Singapore Police Detective (He was one of the officers who said that the description of the hanging device was just a preliminary finding. He was also present when Khal could not describe the external hard drive and did not know its serial number or the make and model.)
- **Traci Goins**: Senior Vice-Consul (Claiming diplomatic immunity, but was present at the interview where Detective Khal gave the initial suicide description.)
- **Craig Bryant**: U.S. Consul (Claiming diplomatic immunity, but was present when we challenged the police on the hard drive and they admitted that the suicide description was not true.)

On May 14, Rick wrote Gloria another email asking her to appeal to the judge for Traci and Craig's testimony. These two emails prove we requested their testimony and were told that they could not do so because of diplomatic immunity. Later, U.S. Embassy Public Affairs Officer, Eric Watnik, publicly denied that diplomatic immunity was ever invoked. He further stated that the embassy had offered Craig and Traci's testimony to our legal counsel and to the state, but both had rejected it, yet another inexplicable example of duplicity on someone's part.

On May 9, just four days before the inquest was scheduled to convene, we finally received the evidentiary package from the state. We were overwhelmed by the amount of information dumped in our laps at the last minute. There was no way either we or our lawyers could sort through it all before the inquiry. The one thing I did examine right away was the pictures the police had taken of Shane after his death. It was heart-wrenching to see photos of my son's lifeless body lying on his apartment floor. As I scanned the photos, one particularly caught my attention. It was one of Shane hanging from his bathroom door. "How could this be?" I thought, "Khal had insisted that no one had taken pictures of Shane before he was taken down."

In his conditional statement, included in the evidentiary package, Khal explained the photo of Shane hanging: "Special Constable Sergeant Soh Guan Huat, Dennis (SC/SGT Soh) approached me and showed me two photographs of the subject in a hanging position. SC/SGT Soh had taken these two photos with his mobile-phone. I acknowledged these photos and asked SC/SGT Sol to delete these photos from his mobile-phone immediately after sending them to me as he would not require the photos further. Subsequently, I received these two photos on my mobile phone from SC/SGT Soh via the 'Whatsapp' application."

As I examined the picture, there was something about it that seemed very familiar. When I compared the unofficial police picture of Shane hanging on the door with the official picture of Shane lying on the floor after his body had been cut down, the similarities were striking; I realized that the picture of him hanging appeared to have been photo-shopped from the picture of him lying on the floor. Every angle and positioning of Shane's head, body, arms, and legs were identical in both pictures. According to Shirley's contention and all SPF accounts, Shane's feet were flat on the floor when he was found hanging, but the picture of Shane hanging did not show Shane's feet. In it, one leg was cocked to the side and the other one was straight—which was the exact same position of his legs in the other picture. This leg position would have prevented both of his feet from touching the floor. Additionally, in both pictures Shane's shirt was crumpled up, exposing his stomach—which, given gravity, would have been hard to explain in the picture of him hanging on the door.

When I showed the picture of Shane hanging to Shirley, she said that was not how she had found him. She reminded me that she found him leaning forward, with his face straight, not cocked to the side, and his arms dangling at his side. She also reiterated that she had seen a thin cord around Shane's neck, not the towel and strap that was around his neck in the police photographs.

Although the police had previously proven incompetent and dishonest, I never imagined they would go to such lengths to prove suicide. I was overcome by the realization that we were facing a larger and more insidious foe than we had anticipated. I was completely traumatized. In desperation, I emailed several friends asking them to pray that I would be able to sleep and that I would have the peace and strength necessary to go through this painful and dark ordeal. At every turn it was becoming increasingly clear to us that the inquiry would not be an open and honest fact-finding investigation, but rather a confrontation between a powerful and proven Goliath with the goal of suppressing the truth and an inexperienced, but dedicated, team of Davids only wanting to uncover it.

Words cannot describe the relief and comfort I felt when Rick's sister Mary and my brother Richard arrived in Singapore, and then a few days later Chet and Corynne joined us. Richard and Mary immediately started assisting in whatever way they could. They accompanied us to all of our meetings and press conferences, and they helped us sort through and examine the massive amount of information we were given by the state. Their presence was a valuable reminder that we were not alone in this battle.

Chapter 13

THE CHARADE

Saturday, May 11, 2013, two days before the Coroner's Inquiry was to begin, Rick, my brother Richard, Shane's girlfriend Shirley, and I spent the entire day in our condo with Gloria and the legal team preparing a strategy. Shirley was first on the list to testify, so we began to prepare her for what she would face in court. Gloria looked directly at Shirley and explained that she would be asked tough questions and would have to look through the photographs the SPF and morgue took of Shane's body. With three packets of photographs in hand, Gloria instructed Shirley to follow her to the back bedroom. Within seconds of the door closing, we heard heart-wrenching crying and screaming. It was agonizing.

After about 10 minutes, Gloria opened the bedroom door and walked into the living room. With a deflated look on her face, she sighed and told us that Shirley was hysterical and could not look at the photos.

"Why does she have to look at the photos?" I asked. "Hasn't she been through enough?"

Gloria explained that the pictures would be shown in court, and that we wouldn't want Shirley breaking down in the courtroom. She then asked if I would try to calm Shirley down and get her to take a look again.

I couldn't help thinking, "Seriously? You're asking me, Shane's mother, to get his girlfriend to look at pictures of Shane's dead body? Are you kidding me? When is this nightmare going to end?" Nevertheless, I hesitantly entered the bedroom where Shirley was sitting on the corner of the bed with tears streaming down her face, her shoulders heaving up and down. I sat down and gingerly put my arms around her. She released herself into my arms and sobbed. After a few minutes, I framed her face with my hands, looked her in the eyes, and said, "Shirley, I know you can do this. I am going to pray that you will have the strength. I'm not going to leave you. I will be with you every step of the way."

Eventually Shirley agreed, and we sat together and looked at every single picture. It was one of the most excruciating tasks I have ever undertaken. Just recounting this scene reminds me once again of how dark our situation was.

The torture did not end with looking at Shane's pictures. After Shirley and I emerged from the back bedroom—completely drained—Steven Lam, the legal team's senior corporate lawyer, announced it was time for Shirley to practice a mock trial.

I protested, "Does she have to do this right now?"

Steven explained that we didn't have time to wait and that he wanted to see how Shirley would hold up on the stand while being grilled by the state lawyers.

By this time, Shirley was so traumatized she could hardly respond to Steven's harsh interrogation. Her voice was weak, barely above a whisper, as she struggled to answer the rapid fire questions. In the end, Steven concluded that Shirley wouldn't do well in court; she was too timid, and she would probably break under pressure. He determined that we would do well to minimize the number of questions directed towards her.

Reflecting back, I regret that we didn't question this tactic. It was as if we were in a trance. We were so desperate for legal help that we blindly trusted Gloria and her pro bono team. In retrospect, we should have protested and probed, "If the Coroner's Inquiry is truly a fact-finding inquest, as everyone claims, why would Shirley be grilled under oath? Why would she have to be strong merely to tell the truth? And why would the state lawyers try to pulverize her?"

In addition to working with Shirley, Gloria also put effort into preparing me for the media and the courtroom. She said that I was far too outspoken, and that I should let Rick do most of the talking. This directive presented a problem. While Rick is thoughtful and observant, I am much more verbal, so I have an easier time speaking articulately to the media. Gloria instructed me to keep my head bowed. She said I should try to appear like a feeble, grieving mother, rather than the strong, focused, mother-on-a-mission that I was. This pretense did not sit well with me, but because we did not know or understand the cultural practices of Singapore and its legal system, we trusted Gloria's advice. Against my nature, I agreed to appear demure and subservient.

The first morning of the inquiry, Gloria arranged to meet us at our condo at 8:30 in the morning. Chet and Corynne, who had arrived the day before, were waiting out front along with the rest of us when a chauffeur-driven black luxury van pulled up. As we headed to the courthouse, Gloria told us what to expect for the day. She reminded us that the inquest was non-adversarial, and that all parties were on the same side, with the goal of discovering the truth. She did caution, however, that the state was leaning toward a determination of suicide. She also warned us to expect an onslaught of media attention at the courthouse. She emphasized that we were under court order not to make any comments to the press and should not speak to them unless she instructed us to.

In spite of Glory's warning, nothing could have prepared us for the scene at the courthouse. It was like a feeding frenzy, with photographers and reporters pushing one another to get a better view and calling out for comment. Gloria and our legal team surrounded us, as we forged our way through the mayhem into the courthouse.

Our trial was held in courtroom 15, on the third floor. It was not a large room, but it accommodated the limited number of people and press that could attend. All foreign journalists, including those from the United States, had to apply for a license to be able to report, and the state only granted a small number of these. Consequently, investigative journalist Ray Bonner had to attend as a bystander and was not allowed to report on the inquiry. The "48 Hours" crew could only rotate in one person at a time. Our lawyers instructed Rick and me not to relay any information about the proceedings to the press, including Ray. According to Ray and the "48 Hours" team, this restriction on reporting was unprecedented.

The courtroom was set up in a typical fashion, with a raised dais for the judge. Our five member legal team sat to the judge's right. The state legal team, consisting of one chief head prosecutor, one senior prosecutor, and three more prosecutors, sat to the left. Directly behind them was IME's legal team, consisting of one senior counsel, and four lawyers. Rick, Richard, and I sat directly behind our lawyers; the rest of the family was seated behind a low partition with the press and the public. Representatives from the U.S. Embassy sat in a row behind the state lawyers. No cameras were allowed in the courtroom, but a court artist with a sketchpad and colored pencils was present.

At 9:30am sharp, the gavel pounded and the words "All rise," resonated throughout the room. Everyone stood at attention, as the Honorable District Judge Cay Yuen Fatt (the coroner) was announced. The coroner was younger than I expected, with a pleasant, yet serious countenance.

Tai Wei Shyong (Mr. Tai), the chief head prosecutor, began the proceedings by introducing his legal team, Gloria's legal team, IME's legal team, and the next-of-kin. As he prepared to read his opening statement, Mr. Tai looked towards the coroner and stated, "Before I begin reading, Your Honour, I think I should say that this statement summarizes all the relevant evidence which we intend to present in these proceedings, including the evidence provided to us by the next-of-kin."

We were flabbergasted at Mr. Tai's claim that his statement represented our evidence. He had never once spoken with us nor interviewed us about why we believed Shane's death to be a homicide. To our knowledge, he had not even interviewed Shane's closest friends or colleagues at IME.

From the outset, it was obvious that the state never seriously considered nor investigated the possibility of anything other than suicide. Everything in Mr. Tai's opening statement promoted the predetermined verdict of suicide. Later that day, Gloria informed me that Mr. Tai held a more powerful position in the legal system than the coroner himself, and that, in some regards, Mr. Tai could be considered Coroner Fatt's boss. I remember wondering, "How will the coroner make a fair judgment if his superior is only presenting evidence supporting suicide?"

Directly following Mr. Tai's opening statement, Shirley was called to the stand. After she was sworn in, Mr. Tai began: "Miss Sarmiento, I am going to read the [conditional] statement that was given to you. Do you have a copy of the statement in front of you?"

Shirley said she did.

Mr. Tai inquired, "Ms. Sarmiento, are you able to confirm that this is your statement which is signed by you?"

Shirley responded, "Yes."

Mr. Tai asked a few supplementary questions, and then got to the heart of the issue: "Ms. Sarmiento, in your statement, you said that you saw Shane hanging from a black cord. This is in paragraph 34 on page 7 of the statement. I would like to show you two photographs." As Shirley looked at the photos he asked, "Are you able to say whether this is the black cord that you saw on the night of 24 June 2012?"

Shirley replied, "I do not remember seeing this. What I can recall was a black cord. I may be wrong, but this is what I remember."

Mr. Tai: "Are you saying that you are not able to remember whether this was a cord?"

Shirley: "It looked like a cord at the time."

Mr. Tai: "Right, thank you. I have no other questions, your honor."

I was incensed, thinking: "These were the state's only questions for Shane's girlfriend, the one who probably knew him better than anyone in Singapore? No questions about his mental state? No questions about his work at IME? Nothing! What kind of fact-finding inquiry was this?"

One of our lawyers, Mr. Foo Cheow Ming, began the cross-examination by asking Shirley if she had ever heard the name Luis Alejandro Andrea Montes.

Shirley responded, "I have never heard of those names before."

I had not heard the name either until Mr. Tai's opening statement, in which he mentioned that Mr. Montes was the last person to see Shane alive. I did not know at that time why Mr. Foo asked Shirley this question, but it later became very significant.

The rest of Mr. Foo's questions revolved around an exhibit picture of Shane's front door. Mr. Foo asked several innocuous questions such as: "Would it be correct to say that this is the door which leads to the stairs going up-stairs?" "There's a doorknob there; is that correct?" and "Can you recall if this door can be locked—is it a door capable of being locked?" I could not figure out why Mr. Foo thought this was so important, but in the transcript of the inquest, there were four pages of testimony about the door and the lock.

Mr. Foo's remaining questions were related to the way Shirley found Shane's body. He asked about the position of Shane's feet, which Shirley had said were flat on the floor, and about Shirley's testimony that Shane was "purple from his elbow down to his fingers." His last question to Shirley was, "So, from your memory, you would, with quite a high degree of certainty, describe the color [a]s purple?"

Shirley responded: "Yes, that's what I remember."

Mr. Foo then concluded, "Thank you very much, Your Honor. That's all the questions I have for Miss Shirley."

Our whole family was shocked that Mr. Foo had asked such weak questions, and I thought to myself, "This is crazy! Shirley just told the state attorney that the SPF pictures of Shane did not reflect the way she found him, and our own attorney only asked about the door, the doorknob, and the color of Shane's body."

The second person to take the stand was, Michael Goodwin, Shane's flat mate. Shane and Mr. Goodwin occupied two separate apartments on the same floor with a common entry. Mr. Tai read Mr. Goodwin's conditional statement and concluded, "I have no questions at this point in time, your Honour."

Although Mr. Tai didn't question Michael Goodman's conditional statement, there were several points that certainly warranted further inquiry.

Mr. Goodwin's statement began:

> On 24 June 2012 (a Sunday), I returned to the property at about 4:30 PM, after having gone to Bangkok, Thailand for a business trip. I had returned to Singapore at about 4:10 PM that same day. The common main floor on the second floor of the property, through which everyone had to pass to reach the apartments on the second floor (the "common main door"), was locked. After using my key to unlock the common main door to access the second floor, I then closed it behind me. However, I left it unlocked. I then went straight to my apartment.

Reading this introduction left me with several questions, "Why would Michael Goodwin emphasize the door being locked, and using the key to unlock it, and how he left it unlocked? Did the police prod him for that information? Was that related to Mr. Foo's questioning of Shirley?"

The next few lines of Goodwin's statement were about the internet password:

> Subsequently, I wanted to access the internet from my apartment. To do so, I needed the wireless password. Although we shared usage of the internet, the internet subscription together with the password was under Shane's name. As I could not remember the password, I sent a text to Shane about 5:33 PM, asking him for it. Shane usually informs me whenever he changes the password and I believed I had forgotten to write down the latest password. Shane was the one who had set the internet password and there was one occasion where he informed me that he had changed the internet password. I believe I had written down the password on a piece of paper but I think that I lost the paper. That's when I came back from Bangkok, I was unable to access the internet and I thought that Shane might have changed the password. So I sent him a text message, asking him for the password. However he did not reply.

I wondered why the state prosecutor did not follow up with more questions about their shared internet access and Goodwin's possible access to Shane's computers. The issue of passwords and access to Shane's computers would have been important to investigate in a homicide case, especially considering that the police had found a sticky note identifying the password. They used this password to open the computer where they said they found the suicide note.

Mr. Goodwin also described his response to Shirley's discovery of Shane's body. He explained that on the evening of June 24, 2012, he heard the common door open and close and assumed that it was either Shane or his girlfriend Shirley. He said he continued working and commented that the door to his apartment remained closed. He stated as follows:

About 20 seconds later, I heard a woman screaming. The woman was asking and crying for help. I open the door of my apartment and saw that it was Shirley who was screaming. I quickly approached Shirley and tried to calm her down. Shirley, however, kept repeating, "Shane, go look, go look." However, I did not enter Shane's apartment. I somehow knew that Shane was dead and that I did not want to see his body. I guess it was just my instincts. Given the severity of the scream, I had assumed that something bad had happened and seeing that would permanently scar my mind. That coupled with the fact that Shirley was a nurse, if she was not attending to him, means that there was nothing she could do and thus my assumption that Shane was dead.

I was astounded by this account, "What person in his or her right mind would not run to see what was wrong with Shane? Shirley never said he was dead, she begged for help. How in the world did Michael Goodwin come to the conclusion Shane was dead? "

The next witness, Ali Miserez, was a close friend of Shane's. Mr. Miserez reported that Shane was not happy with his job and that he was looking forward to returning home, but that he never saw signs that Shane was depressed. When asked, "Could you tell us a little bit about Shane Todd's personality and character?" Ali responded, "He was—he was a solid guy, you know. He was—yes, he was—I mean, he was a good guy. He was professional. He was ambitious, in a good way. He was committed. He was committed I think for his work and for his friendship in general… He had ambition for his life."

The witness that followed, Bart Lendrun, was another friend of Shane's. He testified that Shane never acted depressed. Mr. Lendrun also reported that Shane's lease was to end shortly before his scheduled flight back to the United States, so Shane had made arrangements to stay at his apartment for a couple days.

After the lunch break, Staff Sergeant Ang Yew, one of the first responders to the death scene, took the stand. Sergeant Yew's testimony was important, because it confirmed Shirley's testimony that Shane's body was found hanging from the door with his feet flat on the ground. This again ratified the inconsistency with the staged photo of Shane hanging from the door that I related in the previous chapter.

Sergeant Hua also testified that when he arrived at the scene Shane was lifeless: he did not have a pulse, his body was stiff and cold, and hardened mucus was hanging from his nose. Following this account, our lawyer Mr. Foo questioned, "Did it occur to you, witness, that the subject was moved and the crime scene altered before the arrival of the forensic team and the official photographer?"

Sergeant Hua responded, "Sorry, what actually are you asking?"

Mr. Foo repeated the same question somewhat differently: "Yes, I'm asking: when ASP Tan ordered SC Sgt. Soh Guan Huat to cut the subject down from the door, did it occur to you that he ha[d] caused the crime scene to change before the arrival of the forensic team and the forensic photographer?"

Hua responded: "No, Your Honour"

I was encouraged by this exchange; Mr. Foo was finally asking a strong question. However, he only asked one more pertinent question when he inquired whether the SPF had dusted for fingerprints, or done anything to preserve the crime scene, to which Sergeant Hua responded, "I don't remember." And, again, there was no follow up as to why normal police procedures were not observed.

Before Coroner Fatt adjourned for the day, Mr. Tai requested to clarify a statement he had made in his opening regarding keyword searches relating to suicide on Shane's laptop computer. Mr. Tai stated, "I should have made it clear that these keyword searches were actually searches that were done by the police forensic department in order to find the relevant webpages on the laptop. They were not searches made by him [Shane]. I think there might have been some misunderstanding about this. So, to simplify, the police forensic departments made the searches in order to see whether there were any relevant web searches on these issues on the laptop computer."

By the time Mr. Tai made this amendment, it was too late, the press had gotten word of Shane's alleged suicide searches on his computer, and it was already in print. Every single paper in Singapore featured headlines about Shane's depression and suicide searches. Not one of them mentioned that Shane's friends testified under oath that Shane did not seem depressed and that he never mentioned depression or suicide.

That evening as we read the skewed news reports about the first day of the inquiry, I emailed friends and family to caution them about the bad press and tell them not to be discouraged, even as we struggled to keep our own spirits up.

The following day (Tuesday), we heard several more testimonies from various SPF officers. One of the most telling statements came from Senior Station Inspector, Rayme Darman Koh, who testified that during the course of his career he had investigated about 100 suicides. Prompted by my brother Richard, our lawyer Mr. Singh asked Koh, "Of this 100 suicides, if you can recall, how many turned out to be suicides?"

Inspector Koh replied: "Your Honor, I wish—I would like to state that—I would like to say that all the cases that I have attended are indeed suicide, Your Honour."

This statement further substantiated our suspicions that the SPF never seriously investigates any apparent, but unconfirmed, suicide as anything other than suicide.

One of the hardest testimonies to sit through was that of Ms. Lim Chin, the director of the forensic chemistry and physics laboratory of the Health Sciences Authority. Ms. Lim spent nearly three hours testifying how it would have been possible for my six-foot-one son to tie a noose around his neck with a very small buckle, place it behind the standard-size door, close the door, stand on a chair in front of the door, and jump to his death. She never did explain in any scenario, however, how the chair would have been left upright, a few feet from the door as the police had actually found it.

The coroner allowed Ms. Lim to go into such great detail, that at one point she took 15 minutes to discuss the fiber of the strap, comparing it to the fiber of other straps. She used a suitcase filled with rocks to simulate Shane's body hanging from his bathroom door. Despite her exhaustive testimony, it is still hard for me to fathom how anyone could believe that someone Shane's height could possibly hang himself from a standard size door. Several times, I was so exasperated that I had to leave the courtroom and walk the circumference of the courthouse.

Our son John's arrival in Singapore that evening was a comfort. After such a discouraging day, he brought much needed moral support.

On Friday, May 17, Patrick Lo, Shane's boss from IME, first testified. Mr. Lo looked like he had received a makeover since the last time we saw him. His hair was dyed black, he had lost weight, and he appeared confident. After hours of testimony, however, he became more subdued. On several occasions during his testimony, Mr. Lo lied while under oath and we later found out that he had also encouraged IME employees to do the same.

Mr. Lo first committed perjury with his description of the partnership between IME and Huawei. When asked under oath whether "the purchase of the MOCVD machine [was] made in anticipation of a collaboration or a project with Huawei?" Mr. Lo answered, "No, definitely not." When confronted by our attorney with the evidence from Shane's external hard drive that there was indeed a long-term relationship between IME and

Huawei in terms of the MOCVD machine using GaN technology, Mr. Lo was visibly shaken.[18]

Mr. Lo again gave false testimony when asked about Shane's relationship with the GaN project. Mr. Lo stated that Shane was not the leader of the GaN group; he led that group himself. This contradicted evidence found on Shane's external hard drive, which showed that Shane was in charge of hiring scientists for the GaN group and giving PowerPoint presentations as the GaN group's head. There were also documents identifying Shane as the GaN group leader.

Before going to Veeco for training on the MOCVD tool, Shane had told Dylan that IME had asked him to handwrite special recipes for the machine. Patrick Lo categorically denied that this was true; he stated that there had never been any handwritten recipes. Furthermore, he maintained that it wasn't even possible to hand write the recipes. When confronted with a document found on Shane's hard drive titled "Work Project Proposal" that read, "Veeco has also stated that they will not directly transfer the best-known method recipes to our tool, rather we will copy the recipe details firsthand during our visit to Somerset," Mr. Lo dismissed it by saying that Shane had written that proposal himself. However, we later found an email from Lo asking Shane if he had copied the recipe as instructed.

During his testimony, Mr. Lo also claimed that the MOCVD machine was very common. He likened it to a pressure cooker and said there was nothing special about it. This statement was later proven false when a Veeco representative testified under oath that this particular MOCVD machine was one-of-a-kind, specially made by Veeco for IME.

If the MOCVD machine was so common, as Mr. Lo claimed, it is unclear why IME would need to sign a US export license, as evidenced in Mr. Lo's following testimony:

Question: Dr. Lo, is the MOCVD machine that Shane was involved in purchasing capable for use in military or defense related application?

---

18 My brother Richard put together a timeline with links to documents found on Shane's hard drive demonstrating IME's relationship with Huawei, which is posted at www.justice4shanetodd.com.

Answer: Well, our interest is trying to do the commercial application. One of the strong objectives of this one is to do the power electronic device, you know, so, yes we never sought the military aspect of it.

Question: So I take it that the answer is a "yes." It is capable of being used for military related or defense related application?

Answer: It is capable of doing this. As I mentioned, save for an RF [radio frequency] device, if you are making the device in certain frequencies, but I think there is a license that we signed. We cannot do the military applications.

Question: A license? You mentioned a license?

Answer: Yes, the tool comes with a US export license.

Question: Am I right to say that this machine was sold to IME subject to export control laws imposed by the United States?

Answer: That is correct.

I wasn't surprised that Patrick Lo perjured himself in the courtroom that day. What I couldn't believe was the latitude the court gave him to do so. Never once did either group of lawyers challenge his inconsistencies. I sat there, numb, wondering why we were putting ourselves through the torture of this inquest, when it was clearly a legal charade and not at all a fact-finding inquiry.

Chapter 14

THE NEXT-OF-KIN WALK OUT

O n Friday, May 17, 2013 the Coroner's Inquest adjourned for the weekend. The break provided a much needed reprieve from the courtroom. Our son Dylan arrived in Singapore on Saturday, so we finally had a complete support team of all three sons and our daughter-in-law. While Rick and I attended meetings and approved press conferences, my brother Richard and Ashraf Massoud, the computer forensic expert, created a timeline from documents on Shane's external hard drive proving that Huawei and IME had a lengthy, ongoing business relationship in spite of their denials.[19]

On Monday, May 20, Rick and I arrived at the courthouse early to ensure that the video feed was set up to accommodate the live testimony from Dr. Edward Adelstein, the U.S. pathologist who (based on the autopsy report and photographs of the body) concluded that Shane was murdered. We were dismayed to find the court technicians standing around acting like they didn't know what

---

19   This timeline and the documents that support it can be found at www.justice4shanetodd. com.

to do—as if they had never before set up a satellite testimony. Rick tried to take charge and show them what to do, but no one would listen to him. By the time Coroner Fatt entered the courtroom, the video feed was still not ready, so he ordered that Dr. Adelstein's testimony be rescheduled for the following morning. This concerned us. Dr. Adelstein's wife was having surgery the next day, so we weren't sure if he would even be willing to testify at that time.

After the coroner postponed Dr. Adelstein's testimony, the lead state prosecutor, Mr. Tai, called Patrick Lo, Shane's boss, back to the witness stand. After being confronted with undeniable evidence by our attorneys, Mr. Lo ultimately admitted Huawei's involvement with IME and their use of the MOCVD machine and GaN growth research—an obvious violation of the U.S. export licensing agreement IME had signed regarding the machine. But the court never once addressed the issue of Lo's perjury.

Near the end of the day, Ashraf Massoud was called to the witness stand. Ashraf began his testimony by referring to the forensic report on Shane's Hewlett-Packard (HP) and Gateway laptops prepared by Assistant Superintendent of Police, Soong Yen Peng (Ashraf had to refer to the data in Peng's report because the SPF had not given him access to Shane's computers). Ashraf pointed out that, based on Peng's report, the SPF handling of Shane's laptops grossly violated standard international protocol for preserving digital evidence. He explained that, because digital evidence is volatile and can be changed easily and quickly, the number one priority of any investigator should be to immediately "protect the state of that digital evidence." Ashraf recounted the standard procedure taught by the International Association of Computer Investigative Specialists, a group that provides forensic training all over the world:

On a desktop you pull the plug from behind the tower, so the machine shuts down immediately thereby freezing in that moment in time what files were opened, and what the machine was doing and things of that nature.

And a laptop, of course, we know it has a battery, so you have to pull the battery out immediately to freeze the moment in time of the laptop—in its state at that time.

Then, once you do that, you have to properly image the data, the hard drive, and as I said in my conditional statement, you attach the hard drive to what is called a "write blocker." It prevents Windows, it prevents my forensic machine from altering the data; it blocks any kind of activity to the hard drive; therefore, [you] can't change anything.

Once that is done, you do all the work on the image copy and you never touch the live or the original hard drive again, thereby if anything happens to the image [you] can always go back to the original, and re-image it and do [your] work again.

Ashraf related that—according to the SPF's own forensic reports—they had failed to follow this standard operating procedure. Even worse, the investigating officer had tampered with Shane's laptops, and did not hand them over to a forensic unit for analysis until August 3, 2012, well over a month after Shane was found dead. This compromised the security and validity of any data found on those laptops, making them essentially useless to the investigation.

When the family's attorney, Mr. Ong, asked the question, "Do you have any examples that there is a consequence of not following such protocol?" Ashraf pointed out that the SPF forensic report on Shane's Gateway laptop showed that five files were accessed on June 27, 2012. This was during the time that the investigating officer (IO) had possession of the computers, meaning he was searching the computer and compromising the data. Furthermore, one of the five files the IO had accessed, called "Pros Cons.odt," included the heading "IME" and subheading "Cons," under which Shane had written "possibility of violating U.S. export control laws in project."

In his conditional report, Ashraf also discussed the mysterious files that were accessed on Shane's external Seagate hard drive on Saturday, June 23, the day before his body was found, and again on Wednesday, June 27, three days after his body was discovered—including the Microsoft Office Temporary file that was opened and appears to have been manually deleted.

The following morning, Tuesday, May 21, the courtroom was set up and ready to take Dr. Adelstein's video streamed testimony since he had graciously agreed to testify even though his wife was undergoing surgery. We were anxious to see how the state lawyers would respond to Dr. Adelstein's conclusion of homicide.

Dr. Adelstein's testimony, to say the least, did not go well. The video stream was spotty at best, and Dr. Adelstein seemed muddled and confused. He still contended that Shane was murdered for several reasons: his lung weight, the lack of blood staining on the face, the evidence that Shane was packing to come home, etc. But he changed his initial assessment that Shane had been garroted and then hanged from the door. Instead, he conjectured that Shane could have been murdered in a different manner.

We were disturbed and didn't understand why Dr. Adelstein had modified his original assessment. Following the inquiry, however, we discovered that just prior to his scheduled testimony the SPF sent Dr. Adelstein an 89 page document that included altered pictures of Shane's body. On the front page of the document was the unauthorized "cellphone" picture of Shane hanging from the door, along with a few pictures of Shane's hands and neck. In these pictures, Shane's hands and neck were lily-white and did not bear the defensive marks and scratches contained in the original pictures of his body, which Adelstein had viewed in making his original assessment.[20] In fact, the pictures did not even show the moles on Shane's neck—a clear indication that they had been doctored.

The document also included several pictures of other suicides by hanging and descriptions of how Shane could have hanged himself. We believe receiving this document at the last minute explains why Dr. Adelstein seemed so confused. It may also be the reason the court technicians were "unable" to set up the video feed on the day Dr. Adelstein was originally scheduled to testify. Although the SPF required Dr. Adelstein to sign a privacy agreement saying he would not discuss or release the document, an anonymous unrelated third party gave it to us. The SPF also provided what must have been a similar document and pictures to two American pathologists, whom the state had engaged to testify. On the basis of the supplied pictures, the descriptions of possible suicide scenarios, and a supposedly handwritten suicide note (which we have never

---

20 A comparison of the original pictures with the altered pictures that the police sent to Dr. Adelstein and gave to the two U.S. pathologists who testified at the hearing is available at www.justice4shanetodd.com.

seen), along with the autopsy report, these pathologists concluded that Shane had committed suicide.

In the meantime, Peter Ong, one of our attorneys, flew to Thailand to seek the opinion of the renowned pathologist, Dr. Porntip Rojanasunan. Based on the unaltered photographs taken at the morgue and at the scene of death (that were also submitted by the SPF as evidence to the court), the autopsy report, the pathologist report, and the DNA Profiling Laboratory report, Dr. Porntip concluded that Shane was murdered and that he had fought for his life.

While Peter Ong was in Thailand, Dr. Porntip placed several sticky notes on the photos of Shane with comments such as:

- Abrasions typical of a struggle
- Four signs typical of a hanging not found
  1) Compression of neck veins
  2) Congestion of face
  3) Occlusion of trachea
  4) Protrusion of tongue
- Abrasions atypical of hanging
- Contusion on lips
- No protruding tongue

Dr. Porntip also made the astute observation that, based on the DNA profile report, the towel and the strap contained the DNA of four "unknown persons" (two forms were more pronounced) of "Chinese, Malay or Indian population." More importantly, no DNA was found on the knot or the buckle. The only reasonable explanation for this would be that whoever tied the knot was wearing gloves. Dr. Porntip further observed that the knot in the picture was a fixed knot, not a slip knot, and she attached a sticky note to one of the pictures that read, "Cannot hang yourself via fixed knot."

Dr. Porntip spent several hours on Skype with Peter and Rick explaining her findings and coaching Peter on how to cross-examine the two American pathologists commissioned by the state. We offered to pay her way to Singapore, but she said that the Thai government would not allow her to testify because the political ramifications of this case were far too explosive.

***

After court adjourned on Monday, May 20, Rick, Richard, Ashraf, and I went to Gloria's office to meet with the legal team. While Rick and I were busy talking with the lawyers, Ashraf and Richard were combing through the SPF evidentiary file. All of a sudden Ashraf said to Richard, "You're not going to believe this! I just found an email from Patrick Lo proving that he lied under oath when he denied knowing that Shane had written the GaN recipe by hand during his training at Veeco."

When Richard and Ashraf excitedly showed the email to one of our lawyers, Amarjit Singh, the color drained from Amarjit's face and he rushed out of the room. When he came back some time later (presumably after making a phone call), Richard asked him, "Is this too volatile?" Amarjit responded, "It is way too volatile."

Amarjit's behavior was puzzling. After he left, Richard and Ashraf wondered why the family's attorney would be so reluctant to present evidence that clearly contradicted Patrick Lo's sworn testimony. It was obvious our lawyers were reticent to proceed with this, but we insisted that they enter the email into evidence the next morning, so it could be used in questioning.

***

Following Adelstein's testimony on Tuesday morning, Ashraf was once again brought to the witness stand. Prior to questioning him, our lawyer, Peter Ong, distributed to the court and state attorneys a copy of the email Patrick Lo had written to Shane on January 21, 2012. Peter made it clear that Ashraf had discovered this email in the evidence package tendered by the police. When asked where he specifically found the email, Ashraf answered, "I found it on the DVD labeled 'DVD 4' regarding Gateway laptop, specifically in a folder called 'keyword searches on Patrick Lo.'"

Upon Mr. Ong's request, Ashraf began to read from the email, in which Patrick Lo had written,

Shane, the other thing we need to study (especially Weizhu and yourself) is on the Veeco's Process Recipes (did you get these?).

Shane had replied,

Hi Patrick, Veeco allowed me to take handwritten notes of the recipe details while the process was running. They also said they will send a process engineer to Singapore to help us start GaN-on-SI process.

In response to Mr. Ong's petition to admit this email into evidence, the coroner furiously responded, "I will not admit it at this stage. I made this point time and time again that before you tender documents, to check with the state to confirm the source before you tender documents."

――――――――

Later that evening, in an email to friends and family, Ashraf wrote about the coroner's response, stating,

You know your case is in trouble when the judge will not allow you to introduce evidence that has already been introduced as evidence by the police themselves!!! I was giving testimony today (the prosecution was really coming after me) and I was reading a very damning email that I found on the DVD provided by the police and submitted by the police when the judge stopped me and yelled at the defense for trying to introduce evidence without authenticating the source of the evidence... Mind you, I got this evidence from a DVD that the police had already submitted as evidence.

――――――――

Just when we thought the day in court couldn't get any worse, it did. Right before our lunch break, the state's head prosecutor, Mr. Tai, turned to the coroner and asked,

Sorry, Your Honor, before we break for lunch can I make a request to the court? Earlier at the start of this inquiry I mentioned that there was one witness, a Mr. Luis Montes. As far as we know he was the last person to have seen Shane alive on 23 June. We were trying to bring him down to Singapore and actually we managed to do so because I felt that this was a very important witness. He is ready to give evidence today, but, unfortunately, he is going back to Paris this evening. So I'm just wondering—I'm sorry about this—if we can perhaps interpose him after Mr. Massoud's evidence in the afternoon.

The corner replied, "All right we can interpose Mr. Luis's evidence at 2:30 then. Court is adjourned."

We were shocked and distressed by the announcement of this surprise witness. Although Luis Montes claimed he was the last one to see Shane alive, he was not on the witness list and the state had not provided us with his conditional statement. We were told that he claimed he met with Shane for beer and dinner sometime after 5:00pm on Saturday, June 23, but then couldn't remember where they went.

Based on computer forensic evidence and the fact that Shane did not send any emails,[21] use his cellphone, or respond to incoming calls or Shirley's texts after Friday evening, June 22, we surmised that Shane was murdered either late Friday night, or early Saturday morning, June 23. We were completely astounded that the state would call a surprise witness to discredit our position, without giving us time to vet him or come up with a list of questions. This action was particularly baffling considering that very morning the coroner wouldn't allow us to utilize an email that had already been placed into evidence by the SPF.

Enraged, I told Gloria that I had had enough of this sham inquest. Gloria did her best to calm me down. She suggested that we ask the coroner to delay the testimony of Mr. Montes until the following day, so that we would have time to look into his claims. Gloria and our legal team agreed that if the coroner denied our request, then it was time for us to walk out.

---

21 The last email Shane sent was on Friday, June 22 at 5:16pm. In this email to several friends and colleagues, Shane provided his personal email address and urged the recipients to stay in touch.

After the lunch break, Mr. Tai called Luis Alejandro Andia Montes to the stand. Our attorney Mr. Foo immediately interrupted, saying,

Your Honour, before the witness Luis takes the stand, we have a humble application to make to your Honour. We have been instructed by the next-of-kin to humbly apply for the examination-in-chief and cross-examination of the witness to be held over to tomorrow because the next-of-kin has got ... an excess of evidence to go through with us, so we would really appreciate it if his evidence can be held over until tomorrow."

The coroner replied, "I understand the witness is leaving tonight, so I don't have an option but to put him on the stand and record his evidence. Mr. Foo, you'll have to do the best you can. You can ask all the questions as best as you can."

In response to the denial of our request, Rick, John, Chet, Dylan, Corynne, and I all stood up in unison, bowed to the court, and walked out.

We later learned that Luis Montes had been in Singapore since Saturday, May 18, four days before he was called to testify and that after we left the inquest, the coroner and the state agreed to postpone Mr. Montes' testimony to the following day. Besides not remembering where he and Shane had eaten, Mr. Montes also later reported to one of Shane's IME colleagues that he was not really sure whether he had met with Shane on Friday, June 22 or Saturday, June 23.

Ashraf Massoud wrote the following commentary about our ordeal that day:

The prosecution has been playing games with the family since day one, including examples like saying they would fly me over and then delaying my arrangements for days to the point where the family just finally flew me over. Now the court extended the proceedings another three days (to 5/30) as a tactic to delay the parents from testifying. Well today they allowed a "surprise" witness to testify. In fact, they took me off the stand just for this guy because he had to fly home "tonight"!!! The defense has repeatedly asked for this guy's name and his statement and never got it. This guy claimed to be a very close friend to Shane and had dinner with Shane on Saturday night 6/23, making him the last person to see Shane alive. Yet the family had never heard about him, and even Shane's girlfriend had never heard of him. The family asked for a day delay so they could try to find out who this guy was, and the judge said no and allowed the reading of the witness' statement and the witness to take the stand. The entire Todd family stood up and walked out of the courtroom and never returned… Quite a scene!!! The parents are done with this sham. After the family walked out, now suddenly the witness could stay for another day. We then went right to the embassy and met with the ambassador, but all he could do is give the family lip service. So we're returning, and the family will now plead the case in the court of public opinion to see if they can get any help from our government.

As Ashraf mentioned in his email, after we walked out of court we went to the American Embassy. Our friend Ian Porter, who had also attended the inquiry, followed us to the embassy and acted like a member of the family so he could join our meeting with the ambassador. Ian, an Australian entrepreneur with inventions in the gas and oil industry, had intermittently lived in Singapore and was currently there on business. He had learned about our case through the *Financial Times* article, and was so incensed by the story that he reached out to Rick, offering to assist us in whatever way he could.

When we arrived at the embassy, our entire legal team was waiting for us. We had not invited them to join us, but evidently someone from the embassy had. Ambassador David Adelman, U.S. Consul Craig Bryant, and another high-ranking official met with us in a large conference room. The ambassador was polite, but not as compassionate or concerned as he had been when we first met with him in December. When we recounted what had taken place in the courtroom, he listened and then asked our attorney, Mr. Foo, if what we were saying was true. Mr. Foo answered, "95% true."

Richard and Ashraf then went through the documents showing what had been accessed on Shane's laptops and hard drive after his death, the documents demonstrating an ongoing relationship between Veeco, IME, and Huawei, and the pictures of Shane's undeniable defensive wounds. We also drew attention to Patrick Lo's perjury. All of our points, however, seemed to fall on deaf ears. The ambassador was obviously no longer interested in pursuing the case, as he had asserted he was in December. Once again, we were left wondering what caused the change in attitude.

In an email to a friend, Ian Porter wrote the following about the meeting:

Ambassador Adelman's response to the family after their walking out of the Coroner's Inquiry was ultimately deplorable.

After Richard presented a very convincing and logical sequence of events including hard copy documents supporting a miscarriage of justice, all Adelman could do was offer his sincere condolences.

It was absolutely pathetic what he said next: "We are a powerful country, but we can't interfere in the judicial affairs of other countries."

In the end, I queried if he was comfortable with Singapore being a proxy to the funneling of sensitive intellectual property to a Chinese military connected company. His answer was that the US takes its export control laws seriously and any matter would be looked into accordingly.

After meeting Ambassador Adelman and based on his response, I find him not only ineffectual, but highly involved in what is to my mind a clear cover-up that the Todd family is experiencing.

That evening, as we were preparing to return home, I emailed friends and family explaining, "We walked out of court today and we're not going back. This whole inquiry is a sham. The verdict was made even before Shane was murdered. We are now trying to get back to the U.S. where we can safely tell our story." The deck had been stacked against us before the investigation began.

AsiaOne News sent a crew to film us packing and to report on why we had left the inquiry. I felt sorry for the reporter. Over the last few weeks she had spent a lot of time interviewing us. I could tell from her sympathetic expression that she believed us, yet she knew, and I knew, that she would not be allowed to report the full truth. This reporter was not the only Singaporean who seemed sympathetic to our cause. Whenever we were out, whether walking through the mall or eating lunch, people would recognize us and would give us a thumb's up or would smile and shake their heads up and down in approval. One man actually came up to us at a restaurant and said, "I believe in what you are doing." It was as if these people were grateful that someone was actually trying to take on the Goliath of the state.

The next morning (Wednesday), Rick's sister Mary went to court and Richard headed to the airport for his scheduled flight home. The rest of us weren't able to get a flight until that evening, so we decided to spend the day by the pool. Shortly after we arrived at the pool, however, Ashraf's phone rang. It was the Singapore police telling him that if he did not show up to court that day, he could be held in contempt.

As we contemplated our next move, we noticed that several people dressed in black were covertly taking pictures and video-taping us, so we covered faces with our towels and quickly walked back to the condo. After weighing the options, we decided it would be best for Ashraf to return to the inquest. John, Chet, and Dylan, accompanied him, while Rick, Corynne, and I stayed hunkered down in the condo.

According to the inquest transcripts, Mr. Luis Montes was the first to take the stand on Wednesday, May 22. The lead state prosecutor, Mr. Tai, began by asking, "Mr. Montes, have you met, prior to this inquiry, the parents of Shane, Rick and Mary Todd?"

Mr. Montes said he had and then stated, "I'm not sure about the date, but it was a few days after Shane's death when they came to Singapore. They invite[d] some of their son's friends to their hotel... so I went there with a couple of friends, yes. I don't remember the date to be honest. It was last year."

Mr. Tai inquired, "Did you discuss with them the facts surrounding Shane's death?" Mr. Montes answered, "No, I only told them that I was sorry about [their] son's death, and if I could do whatever I can I will be there. But I just told them that I knew Shane, and he was a good guy and things like that, only that."

Mr. Tai had no further questions. He did not ask Mr. Montes any questions about the night of Saturday, June 23, the night Mr. Montes claimed he had met with Shane for beer and dinner, the night we believe Shane had already been killed.

Next, IME attorney Mr. Jeyaretnam questioned Mr. Montes about the GaN project Shane was working on, which Mr. Montes knew nothing about. Mr. Montes testified that he had attended a meeting with Shane and Huawei, but he was pretty sure nothing ever came of it. Mr. Jeyaretnam concluded by asking, "Are there a number of manufactures of GaN devices that you know of?"

Mr. Montes responded, "A couple of them, but as I mentioned before, I never had a project on Gallium Nitride."

To which Mr. Jeyaretnam expounded, "I'm talking about in the world, there are manufacturers like Sumitomo, RFMD, Freescale?"

Mr. Montes reiterated, "I have read about them and I have heard something as well about them, but as I mentioned, I never work[ed] on a Gallium Nitride project, so I don't know very [much] about this."

When Mr. Jeyaretnam completed his questions, the coroner asked Mr. Montes if the MOCVD machine was intended for military or civilian use. Mr. Montes said he wasn't sure, but he was told it was for civilian use.

Again, neither the state attorneys nor IME attorneys asked Mr. Montes—the last person who claims to have seen Shane alive—any questions about the circumstances surrounding their alleged meeting the evening of Saturday, June 23.

Following Mr. Montes' testimony, Ashraf Massoud was recalled to the witness stand. The state attorneys grilled him for over an hour about the term "last file accessed," trying to excuse the fact that the police had accessed Shane's computer three days after his death. Ashraf later wrote home,

> Okay, so that was intimidating to sit on the stand facing the prosecution and then looking over to the defense table and seeing no one there...
> I just kept harping on the fact that Shane's Gateway laptop computer had been accessed and therefore the data had been compromised

and that any forensic conclusions are now suspect … But they just kept ignoring that and concentrated on things like the definition of the last accessed and Windows 7 behavior, and how close I am to the family, and who else told me to look for these things, etc. This is why the family walked out the other day. They have had enough of the smoke and mirrors and know justice will not be done.

After Ashraf testified, he and the boys stayed in the courtroom to hear Romen Cabillo testify. Romen, a French national, was Shane's close friend and an IME colleague.

Mr. Tai began by asking Romen a series of questions about Shane's mental health, to which Romen responded that Shane was increasingly unhappy at work and was anxious to leave IME, but he had not exhibited signs of depression. Mr. Tai then asked Romen several questions about a meeting on April 11, 2013 between IME director Dr. Kwong, and several IME employees, that Romen had recorded. When Mr. Tai asked whether Romen could recount what happened during this meeting, Romen sarcastically inquired whether he was referring to "the secret meeting called by Patrick Lo."

Mr. Tai reiterated the date of the meeting, and Romen responded, "I was working on that day and then I received a call from human resources. They were asking me to go and see Patrick Lo in his office to be coached about what to say during the latest statement, and I refused to go. I said I don't want to talk about Shane's case with top management of IME because I think it's not legal."

Romen reported that half-an-hour later, a lady from human resources (HR) called him and said, "You must come to the meeting, otherwise you will have to suffer the full consequences."

Romen continued, "Then we went to that meeting that, as I said, was without any mail, any invitation, and we had a meeting with Patrick Lo and I think seven or eight IME employees. And because I was against [going to] that meeting and they forced me to admit [that] if I didn't go I [would] have to suffer full consequences, I [made] the decision to record it."

Romen recounted that, during the meeting, Patrick Lo told the IME employees present that when they made their conditional statements to the police and testified in court they should "consider customer confidentiality," otherwise they could get in trouble and be sued by a company like Huawei. Romen said he argued that "Huawei has absolutely no authority to sue any witness in court."

Later in his testimony, Romen explained that Shane was likely concerned about an organizational conflict of interest in the Veeco-Huawei project. In his conditional statement, Romen wrote, "I think Shane was concerned that the MOCVD system with dual use (for commercial and military purposes) was being used by China." Roman testified, "He [Shane] said to me many times, 'I'm always concerned about US security.' I mean, he didn't go into details about that but he was always very, very, concerned."

John, Chet, and Dylan later reported how impressed they were with Romen. They admired his bravery and honesty throughout his testimony, and because of that he owned the courtroom that day. Romen was later punished for his courage and integrity, as will be explained in the last chapter. In the triumph of corruption and deceit, it is heartening to know that there are still men who will stand for the truth even at personal cost.

Even though our participation in the inquiry had ended, there were still two days left of court. According to Gloria, there would have been five days left if we had stayed because the coroner pushed back Rick's and my testimony until after our original scheduled return to the United States.

On Thursday, May 23, after we had all left, Rick's sister Mary was still in Singapore, so she returned to the courtroom alone to observe the proceedings. The coroner acknowledged her presence and allowed her to ask a few questions. The most significant testimony of the day occurred following her questioning, when a Veeco representative, Mr. Wee, stated that the Gallium Nitrite MOCVD tool Veeco had sold to IME was "customized." There was none other like it in Asia. This contradicted Patrick Lo's earlier claim that the machine was ubiquitous and common throughout the region.

On Monday, May 27, the final day of the inquiry, IME director Dr. Dim-Lee Kwong took the stand. Dr. Kwong, like Patrick Lo, claimed that the MOCVD machine IME purchased from Veeco was common and maintained that Veeco had probably sold 500 of the same tool to China and "the recipe they provided to IME is exactly the same [recipe] they provided to China." His testimony, which completely contradicted that of the Veeco representative, was not challenged.

When asked whether "there is some evidence that Shane was at the very least uncomfortable working with Huawei and that he may have felt he was doing something improper and unethical," Dr. Kwong testified that Shane "only attended one face-to-face with Huawei sometime in April." Again, the documents found on Shane's external Seagate hard drive tell a different story.

Sergeant Muhammad Khaldun Bin Sarif (Khal), the investigating officer at the scene of death, was the last to testify. Khal continued to claim that he had never read to Rick and me the detailed, but inaccurate, description of how Shane allegedly hanged himself. He also again falsely asserted that we had not found Shane's hard drive at the apartment, but that he had given it to us. He stated that he had taken the external hard drive to his office, put it in a metal box, took it out of the metal box, accessed it, and when he found nothing suspicious on it, gave it to me. Khal additionally denied that I had called to ask him about the discrepancies between his detailed description of how Shane hanged himself and the physical evidence I found in Shane's bathroom. Instead Khal stated that I called and asked him to come to Shane's apartment, so I could give him the medication I had found in Shane's medicine cabinet. Throughout his testimony, Khal attempted to portray me as an emotional and confused mother and himself as a competent and upright police officer.

Reflecting back, I think it was appropriate that the Coroner's Inquiry ended with Detective Khal's testimony: It reconfirmed the entire sham of the inquest and why the next-of-kin had walked out. Corruption, deception, intimidation, and lies had always dominated the proceedings, and defeated our pursuit of truth. The one-sided inquest changed the general perception of the case and fighting for truth became increasingly difficult, especially after the coroner published his findings.

Chapter 15

"COMPREHENSIVE, FAIR, AND TRANSPARENT"

A fter returning home from Singapore, Rick and I continued to push our representatives for a congressional investigation and worked to raise public awareness of Shane's case. Knowing that the Coroner's Inquiry worked against us, my brother Richard and his wife Marty—who is also Rick's sister—headed a project to outline and clearly explain the evidence that had been unexamined or ignored at the inquest. Marty wrote an open letter from the family to the media and elected officials, which we widely circulated. The letter provided a brief overview of who Shane was, the research he was involved in at IME, and the circumstances surrounding his death, along with attached supporting files and photographs. Around the same time, our friend, Andy Kasinicky, created the website www.justice4shanetodd.com, so we could more effectively tell our story and display the corroborating evidence. It was all we could think to do to counter the one-sided media reports that had come out of the Coroner's Inquiry.

On Monday, July 8, 2013, our head lawyer, Gloria James-Civetta, informed us that Coroner Chay Yuen Fatt had rendered his verdict. In a 145 page report titled "Findings," Coroner Fatt concluded that the evidence proves "beyond a reasonable doubt, that the deceased committed suicide," that "the evidence was incontrovertibly consistent with asphyxia due to hanging," and that "there was no foul play involved in the deceased's death."

That same day, almost immediately after the release of the Coroner's Report, the U.S. Embassy issued a statement declaring, "The inquiry into Dr. Todd's death was comprehensive, fair, and transparent."[22] This endorsement made the same news cycle as the "Findings," which consequently lent credibility to the flawed and unjust verdict.

We were disappointed, but not surprised, by the coroner's verdict, but nothing could have prepared us for our own embassy's endorsement of the sham inquiry. We were so disheartened that we didn't even read the Coroner's Report.

On Wednesday, July 10, less than two days after the coroner issued his verdict, we received an email through justice4shanetodd.com from a man named Michael Dee, who had read the report. Michael Dee introduced himself as an American and permanent resident of Singapore.

We later found out that Michael Dee was a businessman and philanthropist with a long and impressive resume. He had been an investment banker for Morgan Stanley for 26 years and was the company's regional CEO for Southeast Asia (based in Singapore) from 2000-2004. Following his relocation to Houston, Texas in 2004, he was appointed Honorary Consul General for Singapore. Michael and his family returned to Singapore in 2008 where he became Senior Managing Director of Temasek Holdings, Singapore's government-owned investment company. Michael has also been heavily involved in commercial and community life in Singapore.[23]

---

22 United States Embassy Singapore, "Statement by the United States Embassy in Singapore Regarding the Finding of the Coroner's Inquiry on the Death of Shane Todd," July 8, 2013.

23 Michael Dee has served on the high level Economic Review Committee, the board of Singapore Management University, the board of the Economic Development Board, the board of the Asian Civilizations Museum, and the board of the Singapore American School. He has raised hundreds of thousands of dollars for various philanthropic activities to benefit children with life threatening illnesses and the intellectually disabled. For example, he raised funds to send Singapore's Special Olympics team to both the summer and winter World Summer Games and is a co-founder of the Make-A-Wish Foundation (Singapore).

When he first contacted us, Michael Dee explained that the Coroner's Report had left him with many troubling questions. He believed that the conclusions, despite the time involved, the witnesses called, and the pages written were weak, illogical, and inconsistent, and a poor example of Singapore's high quality legal and judicial system. Michael told us more than once that the investigation and inquiry process and the "Findings" were neither indicative of, nor a positive reflection on Singapore.

Of the many people we met because of Shane's case, Michael was the most supportive of Singapore and its legal system, which he had found to be diligent, thorough, and objective. While Michael challenged us on numerous points and had a never-ending stream of detailed and insightful questions, there was no hiding his disappointment with the coroner's "Findings" in proving suicide "beyond a reasonable doubt." His disappointment ultimately extended to the actions, or lack thereof, of the U.S. government in providing transparency and supporting our efforts to find the truth.

After an independent, comprehensive, and impartial study of the Coroner's Report, Michael wrote a 10,000 word analysis of the "Findings", outlining why, contrary to the U.S. Embassy's statement, the Coroner's Inquiry had not been "comprehensive, fair, and transparent" and suicide had not been proven "beyond a reasonable doubt."

On August 7, 2013, Michael sent his extensive analysis to Singapore's Attorney-General with the following introduction:

Dear Attorney-General Steven Chong,

I am writing you regarding the Coroner's Inquiry for Shane Truman Todd. Pursuant to the Coroner's Act (Chapter 63A) Section 26(3), I am requesting a reopening of this Coroner's Inquiry. As there is no appeal, the coroner takes no questions, the transcripts are not available and the personal effects of Shane are still in police possession, the only procedural route left is to make the case to you that "further investigations are required." I do hope you will give this due consideration.

When the Coroner's Findings were released on July 8, I read it as I had been following the case with passing interest... As I read the report, the questions and anomalies began to stack up, raising numerous questions as to the initial investigation, the completeness of the inquiry and the veracity of the findings. As I began to note these issues into a list, they grew into a long list of questions unasked and unanswered. When the *Strait Times* editorial was published on July 17th, it was clear they had neither digested this report nor spent any time understanding the situation and getting to know the family. I then sought to provide an "Analysis of the Shane Todd Coroner's Findings" which grew into a 26 page, 10,000 word document, which I have attached.

As there are no transcripts, I have solely worked off the Coroner's Findings and public quotes... Please understand I am a friend of Singapore and have always identified with the high standards to which Singapore holds itself and the strong sense of accountability amongst its public officials. Perhaps this was why I was so surprised and disappointed with this investigation, inquiry, and report... I hope you and your staff will read the details of the analysis...

Michael Dee

The remainder of this chapter is an abridged and slightly revised version of Michael Dee's analysis, reprinted with his permission.[24]

Following the release of the Coroner's Report on Shane Todd's death, the *Straits Times* (One of Singapore's 100% government owned newspapers) ran an editorial titled, "Recognizing the Truth in the Shane Todd Case." This editorial maintained that the coroner's findings put to rest the controversy over Shane Todd's death and criticized the family for pursuing further investigation. However, a reading of the Coroner's Report raises more questions and highlights more issues and anomalies than it answers.

---

24 The complete text of Michael Dee's analysis is posted at www.justice4shanetodd.com. After Michael Dee completed his analysis of the Coroner's Report, he distributed it to selected officials involved in the case. Since then, nothing he has written, even a year later and with dissemination by us on the website, has been answered conclusively or proven wrong.

While some of these answers may be found in the transcripts of the Coroner's Inquiry, the transcripts have not been made available to the family and public as required by Section 43 of the Coroner's Act or the coroner's directive to the state counsel on page 12 of the Coroner's Report. These require the coroner and the state counsel to make available the full transcripts, and documents to the family, counsel, and the Public Prosecutor (i.e. the Attorney General). However, the inquiry ended on May 27, and after more than two months the transcripts have not been provided to the Todd family despite repeated requests.[25] This is inexcusable, as one would assume the coroner had transcripts available to write his report. As such, the delay follows in a pattern identifiable from the time Shane's body was found, which only fuels suspicions.

Thus, at this time, the Coroner's Report is the only document of record available to evaluate, and it does not live up to Singapore's standards, nor should it satisfy the Todd family. According to the Coroner's Act, the coroner's role is to determine "how, when and where the deceased came to his death." This analysis contends that this has not been proven or demonstrated.

After a ten-day inquiry, the coroner declared the cause of Shane's death as suicide "beyond a reasonable doubt" and the U.S. Embassy, upon the release of the report, immediately declared the inquiry "comprehensive, fair, and transparent." Local officials have widely used the U.S. Embassy statement to consider the case closed. However, a review of several issues of concern in the Coroner's Report demonstrates why the coroner, the U.S. Embassy, and the *Straits Times* got it wrong.

It should be noted at the outset, that the Coroner's Report and the *Strait Times* editorial depict Mary Todd as a hysterical, anguished, over-wrought, emotional mother on the verge of a breakdown and in denial. Nothing could be further from the truth. Having gotten to know Mary Todd, I would describe her as a strong, determined, rational, loving mother of four sons (now three), supported by a very close family and a deep religious faith. She is not a woman

---

25 Although the state counsel was directed to provide us with the Coroner's Inquiry transcripts, they gave us no indication when we could expect them in spite of our repeated requests. We finally received the transcripts by mail more than 3 months after the inquest, but they were completely disorganized and out of order. We immediately put them in order and scanned them to PDF files, but the hard copy of the transcripts has since been stolen as we will explain in the last chapter.

looking for sympathy, pity, condolences, or comfort. She is a woman who wants the highest good, the truth.

———————————————

Reading the Coroner's Report, one notes a defensive tone, questionable judgments, conflicting testimony, loose ends, and spurious opinions. The Coroner's Report goes beyond its purpose and seeks to rebut contentions of the family and the media across a wide range of issues, many unrelated to the cause of Shane's death. After more than a full year, crucial questions still remain unanswered—hence, the family's rejection of the report's conclusion.

The *Straits Times*, the government's newspaper of record, portrayed the Todds as having "turned their backs on the proceedings." To the contrary, the Todd's walked out of the inquiry about halfway through on matters of principle and in protest against the unfairness of procedure. Their frustration began when they received documentation (the SPF evidentiary bundle) too close to the inquiry to fully review its contents prior to the proceedings. Their frustration built when the coroner changed the original date of their testimony to beyond their scheduled time in Singapore, thus precluding their testimony without significant hardship. It culminated, amongst other issues, with the surprise announcement of an important witness not fully disclosed in advance.

This witness, Luis Montes, arrived in Singapore at 7:00pm on Saturday, May 18. The state counsel received his conditional statement at 7:00pm on Monday, May 20, yet the state counsel did not announce that he was ready to give evidence until just prior to lunch on Tuesday, May 21, on the day he planned to testify. The family simply asked for a one-day adjournment to prepare for cross examination and request necessary documents relating to this witness. They allegedly had met this witness briefly at a widely attended gathering almost a year earlier, but they did not remember him. The coroner denied this adjournment request, as he did not want to "inconvenience" the witness who was due to fly to Paris the next day. The coroner blatantly ignored that this witness readily offered to stay an extra day to aid in the cross-examination.

All this is essential, as this witness, Luis Montes, was Shane's friend who claims he spent substantial time with Shane the day before his body was found and was believed to be the last person to see him alive. The coroner wrote, "the confirmation of Luis Montes as a witness was indeed rather late," yet he still refused to grant even a one-day adjournment. Further, while the Coroner's Report stated that Luis Montes met Shane the evening before his death, the family says Mr. Montes later expressed uncertainty as to what evening they actually met.

Furthermore, the report said Luis had gone to Shane's house the day before his death to look at furniture and then they went to a local coffee shop for a beer, made plans to go surfing in California, and discussed the future of CMOS vs GaN technology. Luis testified that Shane was "normal" and gave no indication whatsoever that he was either depressed or suicidal. Just 24 hours later, Shane was found dead. It seems neither fair nor empathetic to deny a one-day adjournment to allow the family to prepare for such a key witness.

One of the more significant aspects of this inquiry affecting the credibility of the investigation are the differing accounts of discussions between Mary and Rick Todd and Investigating Officer Khaldun ("IO Khaldun") over the police description of the scene of Shane's death. Mary Todd claimed IO Khaldun read a detailed description of how Shane hanged himself. It involved a complex scene of holes, bolts, ropes and pulleys. When Mary Todd saw the apartment, it bore no resemblance to the description IO Khaldun had read, so she asked to see the paper he had read from. IO Khaldun later denied he said this, yet refused to turn over the paper from which he was reading.

There was a simple way to determine the truth; Ms. Traci Goins, Vice-Consul at the U.S. Embassy, was present during this discussion, as was Rick Todd, Mary's husband. Thus, to determine who is telling the truth, Ms. Goins only needed to testify or make a conditional statement, yet she did not.

The coroner should have utilized his magistrate's court powers to compel this testimony and establish who is telling the truth. However, the coroner states that "…it was significant to me that the only other person privy to the discussion, namely Ms. Goins, did not provide to the court any reason why she was unable to come forth to confirm if the Next-of-Kin's version of events was indeed true."

The U.S. Embassy has maintained on numerous occasions that the embassy offered Ms. Goins and U.S. Consul Mr. Bryant to testify and to delay Ms. Goins' relocation back to the U.S. to accommodate the schedule of the inquiry. However, according to the U.S. Embassy, the state counsel never requested their testimony. The U.S. Embassy further related that on the last day of the Coroner's Inquiry they were contacted by the state counsel about Ms. Goins' availability, yet, as the state counsel was aware, she had already left the country. On the other hand, the state counsel claims, in no uncertain terms, that the U.S. Embassy never made Ms. Goins or Mr. Bryant available to testify. This is a direct contradiction to the position of the U.S. Embassy.

It is important to ponder this fact pattern. The coroner twice blames Ms. Goins and the U.S. Embassy for her lack of corroborating testimony and unexplained unwillingness to testify. The U.S. Embassy claims she was made available. The state counsel claims she was never made available. Why didn't the coroner demand to get to the bottom of this directly contradictory testimony? Is it a fact that the state counsel never requested her to testify? Or did the U.S. Embassy not make her available? It cannot be both. Someone is lying. This alone damages the credibility of the Coroner's Report.

One should also consider why the family did not call Ms. Goins and Mr. Bryant to testify. According to the family, they have proof of having requested this testimony, yet it seems that the family's counsel, under the advice of Mr. Bryant, informed the family and the state counsel that Ms. Goins and Mr. Bryant could not testify due to diplomatic immunity. The U.S. Embassy has emphatically denied this and the question remains unresolved.

Following on the issue of credibility over the testimony of Ms. Goins and Mr. Bryant, the external hard drive also remains an important outstanding issue. The family testified that they found the device in Shane's apartment a few days after his death and, believing it was a computer speaker, they packed it with his personal effects. Once home, the family realized the device was in fact Shane's external hard drive that had been used to back-up Shane's computer. The family sent it to a specialist in computer forensic examination, who found that it contained a variety of files relating to Shane's work at IME. These files, along with Shane's discussions with his parents, subsequently formed the basis of the family's hypothesis that Shane's was murdered due to his work. This scenario is the one which appeared in the *Financial Times* (FT) article "Death in Singapore" on February 15, 2013.

Is it just a coincidence that on February 27, 2013, only 12 days after the FT article appeared, and 248 days after Shane's body was found, SPF Superintendent Tan wrote the FBI requesting their assistance with this hard drive? Mr. Tan only asked for three areas of cooperation and two were in retrieving and examining the hard drive and providing the analysis to the police. The family offered a copy of the hard drive if the police provided a copy from Shane's computers and phone. The police declined. The SPF's desire to have the hard drive returned was prominently covered in the media, and the family was portrayed as withholding evidence.

Here again we see the disingenuous actions of the police. IO Khaldun testified at the inquiry that he had given the hard drive and two thumb-drives to the family just days after Shane's death. He further testified that he did not seize the hard drive and two thumb drives in the same way that he had seized the computers, the cell phone and IME diary, but rather that he brought them back with him "to the Central Police Division for safekeeping." This raises the question, why did he seize this evidence differently than the other evidence?

IO Khaldun further produced a receipt dated June 28, 2012 claiming that he had provided the hard drive to the family and then acknowledged that he had also accessed this hard drive three days after Shane's body was found. Thus, the SPF story is that they found the hard drive, didn't follow international standards by sending it immediately to the computer forensics department, but rather decided to keep it for "safekeeping," then accessed the hard drive ignoring forensic protocol. After deciding it was a "personal effect," they allegedly gave it to the family, and issued a receipt for it. Some 35 weeks later, the SPF formally requested that the FBI seize and analyze the hard drive, sending the results to the police, but they refused to share the other digital data with the family. In the meantime, they used the media to make it look like the family was obstructing justice. This is baffling, given the SPF claim that they gave it to the family.

Moreover, this hard drive was accessed on Saturday, June 23, at 3:40am the day before Shane's body was discovered, and then again at 5:47pm when he was supposedly having beer with Luis Montes. This anomaly remains unexamined and unexplained by the coroner. It is especially surprising since, according to phone records, Shane's cell phone was not used at all on June 23, which was highly unusual for someone who used his phone frequently.

These discrepancies alone cast doubt on the veracity of this investigation and inquiry, yet many others can be found in the Coroner's Report. For starters, in modern investigations, it is standard practice to review digital footprints as one would fingerprints or DNA. Computer forensics are used to recover the full array of data and thus it is essential to turn over such computers and cell phones immediately to a forensic lab before the batteries drain and lose RAM memory, tainting the evidence. The Technology Crime Forensic Branch of the Technology Crime Division, Criminal Investigation Department of the Singapore Police Force handles Singapore's computer forensics and dates back to 1996. However, Shane's computers and cell phone were not handled according to international standards for reasons which remain unexamined and unexplained by the coroner.

Shane's HP laptop was seized the day his body was found. His Gateway laptop, which was right on top of the TV console, was not discovered for an additional three days. The two laptops were not subsequently sent to the forensic lab until about five weeks later, which is not explained nor examined. This begs the question: Where were they and how were they handled for that five-week period? It further creates the suspicion of, and potential for, tampering with evidence, given the family immediately challenged the assumption of suicide and repeatedly emphasized to the police their suspicion of foul play.

Even more troubling is that the cell phone was not sent to the forensic lab until 78 days after it was seized and 41 days after the laptops were sent for investigation. After the phone was recovered, it was left on until the batteries drained. The phone activity in the period just prior to and following his body being found is not disclosed, yet is highly relevant. The reason for this extreme delay and the handling of this crucial piece of evidence remains unexplored and unexplained in the Coroner's Report. One wonders if this were a criminal trial whether any of this evidence would even be admissible in a court of law, as the evidence was never properly secured. One also wonders about the IME diary that was discovered when Shane's body was found. This was considered evidence, yet was not sent for analysis for 24 days and then only for handwriting. There is no mention of the content of the diary in the Coroner's Report.

On March 12, 2013, the *Financial Times* reported that the Singapore Police and K. Shanmugam, Singapore's Foreign Minister, committed to sharing with the FBI all of the evidence obtained, including the computers found in his apartment. Yet there is no mention of whether this took place, to what extent, and most importantly what conclusions the FBI reached as a result of this sharing, if any. Whether this commitment from the highest levels of the Singapore government was fulfilled remains an open question, yet no information from the FBI is included in the Coroner's Report and it remains unresolved.

The media also failed to report that the coroner rebuked Dr. Lo, Shane's "immediate supervisor at the IME," for "improper influence of witnesses" on April 11, 2013, in relation to their testimony at the inquiry. According to the coroner, "Dr. Lo simply had no right to try to delineate or circumscribe the scope of the witnesses' [conditional] statements" and he was "wrong and ill-advised" for doing so. While this could be considered obstruction of justice, the coroner took no action.

Most fascinating is that IME employee, Romen Cubillo, made a secret audio recording of this meeting with Dr. Lo. The following excerpts from the recording make clear what Dr Lo was attempting to do, and why Romen would feel the need to record the meeting:

Dr Lo: "...in my (statement) we talked with the police about the Huawei project... (not audible). It's only between us and the police. It was not intended to be released in the public. The whole reason that IME is keeping very quiet because there is some confidential information which... we are not supposed to say (not audible)... You read IME statement, respect the customer's confidentiality... (not audible) ...It's the integrity of the A*Star as well as IME... (not audible) so that is the whole reason..... (not audible)... what you need to do (not audible)... You understand what I am saying... you understand?"

Romen: "...I spoke the truth.. I have no issue during the coroner's inquiry if the judge is asking for more details...".

Dr Lo: "...make sure that the things that you say [do] not violat[e] the confidential rules."

Romen: "But the law is above the contract... It's above the contract."

Here we see Romen brought a recording device into a meeting clearly for protection from undue pressure from Dr. Lo, who is trying to affect the testimony of the seven witnesses in the room. Romen demonstrates his unshakable integrity and rightly resists this pressure from his superior.

The coroner went to great pains to paint Shane as depressed and suicidal, despite an overwhelming lack of evidence from friends and colleagues. While he was anxious and unhappy with his work, he was not perceived as either depressed or suicidal.

The coroner used Shane's treatment for depression in 2002, over a decade ago, to create a trail of depression and suicidal tendencies. The coroner wrongly uses treatment from ages ago to try and justify something for which there is no evidence today from people who interacted with Shane—including family, friends, co-workers, and his girlfriend—in the period immediately preceding his death.

The coroner also failed to mention that when Shane reportedly visited his college clinic for depression in 2002, he was studying in graduate school, working as a teaching assistant, and involved in many outside activities. His work load was heavy and time consuming. He subsequently became exhausted and depressed. He then visited an on-campus clinic, in a mature act of concern over his well-being and general health. He visited this clinic only once and received no medication. The clinic agreed that through improved sleeping patterns, a healthy diet, and an increased level of exercise, he would be fine. In short, the Coroner's Report tries to frame the 2002 visit in ways that are not consistent with reality. That Shane saw a qualified physician for depression over a decade ago and then had a single visit in April 2012 is hardly a marker for suicide. In fact, it is a sign of someone who is self-aware, confident, and committed to his personal health and well-being.

The coroner additionally goes to great lengths to discuss suicide websites Shane reportedly visited in the months prior to his death. However, when the family requested the URL's and links, they were not provided. Here one must also keep in mind that the laptops were not properly transferred to a forensic lab for five weeks. Also, it remains unknown, assuming the sites were visited, what other explanation could be considered. Many people have visited some of the same websites generally cited in the report, such as those about suicides off Marina Bay Sands.

Shane saw Dr. Lee, a trained psychologist, on one occasion of unknown duration on April 4, 2012 for a consultation on a "sense of anxiety." Dr. Lee testified that Shane's situation was "moderate" and that Shane "did not feel that life had no meaning nor were there any suicidal ideations expressed." Ignoring this statement, the coroner makes incredulous leaps of intuition about Shane's state of mind, calling into question the objective nature of the report.

The coroner has given extraordinary weight to this single visit with Dr. Lee, well beyond what is warranted, and weaves it into a tale of recurring depression and visits to websites leading to suicide, when all the evidence does not point to suicidal tendencies whatsoever and the computer data cited was compromised, given it was not turned over to forensic authorities for about five weeks.

There are further unresolved discrepancies surrounding the state of Shane's body in the hanging position. The police reported that when Shane was found, his "feet were flat on the bedroom floor." The coroner attempts to explain this based on the 'simulations' performed at the inquest, which admittedly did not use the same materials, and were conducted under conditions and with knots, not verified by other experts. It is additionally unclear to what extent these simulations replicated the actual conditions of Shane's death.

Then there is the matter of the photos allegedly taken at the scene. IO Khaldun claims that when the police arrived at the scene, Special Constable Sergeant Soh took two photos of Shane hanging on the door with a cell phone. These are the only photos allegedly taken of Shane on the door in a hanging position. IO Khaldun ordered the photos be sent to him and then deleted. The Coroner's Report does not mention those photos again. When Mary Todd arrived, she asked IO Khaldun if photos of Shane hanging on the door existed and was told no. Thus, crucial photographic evidence was handled in a haphazard manner and not within professional standards for evidence. The coroner does not inquire into these photos.

Equally important, the evidence in Shane's apartment was not preserved due to preliminary assumptions made by the police. Thus, no fingerprints were ever taken and no DNA was collected at the scene. The police on the scene dispute each other under oath as to whether Senior Station Inspector Rayme was wearing gloves or not when handling the computer. While the coroner does not discuss whether any other police at the scene were wearing gloves, several photos show Shane's body being handled without gloves.

Furthermore, the black strap and white towel against Shane's neck was not sent for forensic testing until 37 days after it was seized. The DNA results showed there were two prominent samples of DNA in addition to Shane's on those items. Singapore has maintained an extensive DNA database for over a decade, yet the coroner made no reported attempt to try and identify the additional DNA and dismissed it as "ultimately neither here nor there." It is quite striking how the coroner makes fantastic judgments about Shane's state of mind on supposition, yet breezily dismisses the hard evidence of alien DNA without any effort to identify it.

Finally, I would note that when Shane was found, his front door was unlocked, and Shane's neighbor mentioned he knocked on the door of Shane's apartment the day of his death because the internet was not working. The Coroner's Report does not discuss these relevant issues of why the internet was out and Shane's front door was unlocked.

While not dwelling at this time on the many anomalies relating to Huawei and IME, it is worth noting that IME had a total of five contracts involving Huawei. They dated back as early as 2007 and, at the time of Shane's death, three were still outstanding and ongoing. IME and Huawei clearly had an established relationship and had been discussing the GaN Power Amplifier Project for over a year until it was seemingly delayed (not canceled). Shane had participated in a meeting with Huawei about the GaN Power Amplifier on April 19, 2012, only

66 days prior to his body being found. Then Huawei and IME held a meeting on June 5, 2012 (without Shane). This was only 19 days before his body was found.

Huawei then seems to have delayed cooperation on the GaN project with IME in an e-mail dated July 11, 2012 saying, "Because our goal of GaN is indeterminate until now, so we couldn't start the cooperation on SiC immediately, let's keep in touch." This email was sent only 17 days after Shane Todd's body was found. An obvious question would be: What is the real meaning of this email, considering Huawei was an established research partner of IME? Also, it remains unexplained and unexplored whether IME told Huawei of Shane's death and exchanged emails or phone calls to this effect.

As to the possibility of violating export controls with the GaN Power Amplifier described in the Coroner's Report, Shane was right to be concerned. Even though the coroner concludes that "there was no basis to have such worries," Dr. Kwong, head of IME, directly contradicted this conclusion when he testified, "…it was general practice in the research industry to research a little beyond the specifications of the required device." The GaN Huawei-IME specifications were 150 watts at 0.5 to 3.0 GHz. If the GHz rating only increased to 3.2 GHz, there would be an export violation. Dr. Kwong testified that "…the frequency and power output of the actual device might be lower than that researched into for the model." Thus, Dr. Kwong admitted that the device might be tested at a level that violated export controls.

The facts so far discussed represent but a few of the many anomalies within the Coroner's Report. Many of these relate to the procedures utilized by the police. Nevertheless, the coroner asserts in his report,

> It is not for me at this forum to make findings on the appropriateness or adequacy of the standard operation procedures of the SPF, or on the conduct of the police officers in carrying out their investigations the way that they did. These are ultimately matters within the remit of the relevant authorities and the internal review mechanism of the SPF. While I accept that the police officers had exercised their discretion to make certain judgment calls in this case (which I found no reason

to disagree with based on the circumstances available in evidence),
there should perhaps be more guidelines put in place and/or enforced
to govern such exercise of discretion.

With this statement the coroner implies that the police either did not
have proper guidelines and/or did not enforce existing guidelines. The coroner
decides not to hold the police accountable for bad judgment, sloppy procedures,
improper handling of evidence, and their divergent statements. This lack of
accountability violates Singapore's hallowed principles of meritocracy, discipline,
and integrity. Here the coroner refuses to discuss in any way those actions by
the police which may have compromised this investigation, which thus fatally
damage the credibility of this report. Without question there should be a full-
scale investigation into the police actions and procedures in this case.

At this point, it's important to step back and look at the bigger picture.
Shane Todd was a highly successful PhD who was unhappy in his work position
for a variety of reasons. He quit his job, got a new one in the U.S., and was
packing to move home in one week. He had clothes in the laundry, boxes on
the floor, price tags on his furniture, and his cell phone charging. He had said
good-bye to his many friends and colleagues and had asked his family to hold
off on a celebration until he got home. The night before his body was found,
he was supposedly having a beer and making plans to go surfing with a friend
in California. He was in a stable relationship and had made plans to continue
that relationship upon his return to the U.S. No one in his wide range of
friends testified to any abnormal or very depressive or suicidal behavior. A
doctor he saw reported no troubling warning signs. Does this really sound like
a suicide scenario?

Now add that he had been ringing alarm bells over the possibility that
classified national security secrets might be being leaked to the Chinese, and
he told his family he feared for his life, showing obvious anxiety. He then acted
on his concerns by giving notice to the IME and finding a new job. This broad
picture, in tandem with the points raised above does not merit a declaration of
suicide "beyond a reasonable doubt."

It is not the role of the family to prove murder and provide a motive. It is, however, the role of the coroner to prove suicide. The Coroner's Report does not offer proof "beyond a reasonable doubt." At best, it can be called inconclusive, but it is certainly not "comprehensive, fair, and transparent" as claimed by the U.S. Embassy. The family and all who are willing to invest time in this case are justified in not believing closure has been reached. The investigation, inquiry and Coroner's Report clearly does not do justice, especially given the severity of this situation and its high profile nature.

Chapter 16

IF SHANE DIDN'T WRITE THE SUICIDE NOTES, HE DIDN'T KILL HIMSELF

n April 2013, before the Coroner's Inquiry was to convene, Rick's sister Marty began encouraging us to hire an expert to examine the alleged suicide notes that Detective Khal said he found on Shane's computer. Initially, I didn't think this was necessary. We already had ample evidence to prove Shane was murdered, and I didn't want to spend any more time or money verifying what I already knew—that Shane did not write the notes. I also naively believed that the coroner would consider, not refute, the evidence of homicide.

In spite of my reticence, my nephew Roston Elwell took the initiative to find someone qualified to analyze the notes. At the time, Roston was taking an online course called "Natural Language Processing," so he asked the professor if he could recommend someone. He was referred to Dr. Carole Chaski, the executive director of the Institute for Linguistic Evidence and developer of ALIAS (Automated Linguistic Identification and Assessment System) technology, a software system used to recognize texts and determine authorship. Roston emailed Dr. Chaski about Shane's case and asked for her assistance. She responded:

Dear Mr. Elwell,

Thank you for your inquiry. I would be interested in working on this case. In fact, I believe that a news reporter has already contacted me about this case. I will read the links you sent me next week. Meanwhile I have attached my CV, fee schedule and an article about my method; since this is a "cold case investigation" I would classify this case at the indigent or law enforcement rate.

Best regards,
Carole E. Chaski, PhD
ALIAS Technology LLC

Roston forwarded us the email, but because Rick and I were so consumed with the inquiry, I did not contact Dr. Chaski until June 10. After a long conversation, Dr. Chaski agreed to analyze the alleged notes and requested that we send additional samples of Shane's writings. She also asked if I had spoken to Dr. David Camp, as he had already contacted her about Shane's case. I told her that I had never heard of him. Dr. Chaski responded that I should get in touch with him, as he had an interesting story to tell me. She promised to introduce us through email.

That afternoon, after our conversation, I received an email from Dr. Chaski saying, "I ran the total note as one document, the first page as one document and the second page as one document through ALIAS SNARE." Dr. Chaski explained that ALIAS SNARE has an 88.6% accuracy rate in distinguishing real suicide notes from control documents (non-authentic suicide notes) and that in both tests, the text of Shane's alleged notes was not classified as a real suicide note, but rather as a control document.

When I asked Dr. Chaski to clarify, she explained that ALIAS SNARE runs a test to determine authenticity by comparing the document in question against a database both of real suicide notes and control documents (ones having similar characteristics to suicide notes, such as apology letters, love letters, simulated or hoax suicide letters, etc.). She related that, according to the test results, Shane's alleged suicide notes were not authentic.

Dr. Chaski later sent us an official assessment titled, "Shane Todd Death Investigation of Alleged Suicide Notes." In this report, Dr. Chaski outlined her methods and listed her main findings, which are as follows:

(a) The alleged suicide note is not a real suicide note;

(b) The fragment from the hard drive alleged to be a suicide note is not a real suicide note;

(c) Known writings of Shane Todd in the months before his death do not contain any indications of real suicide notes or suicidal language;

(d) The language of the alleged suicide note is non-native English, so that the authorship of the alleged suicide note is not Shane Todd, a native speaker of English.

Dr. Chaski concluded her report by stating that, if called as a witness, she could and would testify to these same findings.

On July 5, Dr. Chaski introduced me to Dr. David Camp via email. Dr. Camp is a professor of criminal justice at Blackburn College. He also created the only fully academic college course on deception management (the scientifically proven methods of lie detecting used by federal agents, law enforcement, and other professionals). He is also the founder and senior analyst of EnSol LLC, a deception evaluation and instruction company, and is a founding member of LEADDS (Linguistic Evidence Analysis and Deception Detection Solutions).

Dr. Camp emailed me his phone number, and I immediately called him. After a brief introduction, I asked Dr. Camp how he had heard about our case. He told me that after the *Financial Times* article came out, Jeremy Wagstaff, the Chief Technology Correspondent for Reuters in Singapore, had emailed him seeking his expertise in analyzing suicide notes. I was stunned by this information. As mentioned in chapter seven, Wagstaff was the reporter whom Rick and I had contacted through a friend. Wagstaff had initially seemed interested in pursuing our case and I had sent him the suicide notes and other emails from Shane. But after some conversations with IME employees, Wagstaff coldly informed us that he had not found compelling evidence to suggest foul play and believed Shane's death to be a suicide.

Dr. Camp explained that Wagstaff had sent him Shane's alleged suicide notes along with several of Shane's writings and asked him to analyze them. (These were obviously the documents we had privately sent him.) Wagstaff ended his request by saying, "Thank you in advance, and [let me know] whether you need more information. Needless to say, I'd appreciate it if you could treat the material as confidential and limit its circulation."

Dr. Camp agreed to analyze the suicide notes in comparison to Shane's other writings for no fee, and told Wagstaff that he would also consult with a colleague, a certified court approved forensic document examiner, Dr. Carole Chaski.

A few weeks later, Dr. Camp sent Wagstaff a ten page analysis of the suicide notes, concluding that Shane had not written them, the cultural references in the note clearly indicating that the author was from an Asian or Middle Eastern upbringing. Wagstaff never responded to Camp's detailed analysis. It would seem that the conclusion did not fit the narrative Wagstaff was seeking to prove, as he never thanked Dr. Camp for his help or wrote anything about it for Reuters.

At our request, Dr. Camp published an official report concluding that "the main piece of evidence for the determination of suicide (the suicide note) was not written by Shane Todd and thus his death <u>was not</u> suicide."[26] According to Dr. Camp, when writing a genuine suicide note, an author generally follows certain patterns. In his report, Dr. Camp listed the indicators and attributes of suicidal association, along with an explanation of how these patterns and signs were not present in Shane's verified personal communications before his death. He wrote:

1. **Unbearable Psychological Pain**: The closest inference to such a perception is a brief reference to the subject's friends concerning the unethical practices he had concerns about. This is not sufficient to meet the criteria implicated in the category. If this were a real indication of

---

26 David Camp's entire report titled, "Shane Todd: Document Analysis: Is there Support of Suicide as a Manner of Death," is posted at www.justice4shanetodd.com.

such, the documents would have placed much more time and space on the topic and included wording emphasizing the problem in emotional terms. This indicator is weakly supported.

2. **Problems with Interpersonal Relations:** There are no indications of interpersonal relational problems whatsoever. There is no identifiable support for this attribute.

3. **Rejection/Aggression:** There is no indication of intent or wording that suggests any emotional concerns that could be considered as a precursor to such intent. There is no identifiable support for this attribute.

4. **Inability to Adjust:** There is no indication of such an inability. However, there are very specific indicators that the subject is looking forward to changing circumstances. There is no identifiable support for this attribute.

5. **Indirect Expressions:** As previously indicated, the wording provides no examples, allusions, inferences or references suggesting such. There is no identifiable support for this attribute.

6. **Identification Regression:** The subject provides multiple instances indicating the presence of a strong ego and a balanced ego structure. His numerous friendships and the contents of the communications related to those relationships indicate a strong positive set of expectations toward upcoming events. There is no identifiable support for this attribute.

7. **Cognitive Construction:** In verified suicide notes and psychological reports the existence of a narrowly focused cognition, especially in relation to the lack of alternative opportunities (hopelessness) are expected. The documentation provided indicates no such narrowing of focus or concerns and in fact suggests the subject was looking forward to the opportunities awaiting him already in evidence. There is no identifiable support for this attribute.

Dr. Camp summarized, "In short, these well-established indicators suggest a complete lack of suicidal ideation and lead to a conclusion that suicide was not previously considered."

When comparing the writing style of the suicide notes to the style in Shane's verified written communications (submitted personal emails), Dr. Camp explained, "A person who has been literate for much of their life develops a style of writing that is consistent throughout their communications." The comparison between the alleged suicide notes and Shane's other writings strongly indicated that Shane was not the author of the notes. For example, the average number of characters per word and sentences per paragraph were significantly different in the alleged notes compared to the examples of Shane's verified writings. Furthermore, based on the Flesch-Kincaid Grade Level Test, which rates a text to a U.S. school grade level, the suicide notes were written at a significantly lower grade level than Shane's other communications.

Lastly, Dr. Camp engaged in a content analysis of the notes and concluded, "The consistent outcome was not only that the suicide note was not written by Shane Todd; it was not written by a person who was socialized in the same culture or with the same linguistic patterns. More specifically, the indications are that the note was written by a person who has learned or uses English as a second language and who had access to personal information about Shane Todd, although such information was incomplete and error prone."

While I was initially hesitant to have the alleged suicide notes analyzed, I am grateful for the professional confirmation that my son did not kill himself. To the average person, Shane's case is extremely complex and hard to comprehend. Many people are baffled by the question of why anyone would want to murder him—what would be the motive? The GaN technology Shane was working on, and the illegal transfer of it, is not easy to understand, much less explain.

What is simple and easy to understand, however, is that if Shane did not write the suicide notes, he did not kill himself. Dr. Camp and Dr. Chaski's analyses are useful in this regard, but they merely scientifically confirm what I, as Shane's mother, knew and expressed the moment I read those notes in that small, dark room at the Singapore police station: "My son did not write these notes."

Chapter 17

WHAT ARE THEY HIDING?

Since learning of our son's tragic death in Singapore, Rick and I have relentlessly sought to discover the truth about what happened to him. We never could have imagined how difficult that quest would be. Over the past two years, we have uncovered evidence indicating that Shane quit his job because he was concerned about U.S. security, and that doing so cost him his life.

At every step, we have faced inexplicable obstruction, even from those who should have been our advocates. The Singaporean state, judicial system, and police force have opposed us; IME and Huawei have opposed us; and our own State Department has opposed us. We have been ignored, stonewalled, lied to, lied about, and publically smeared. The Asian press has portrayed us as emotional, irrational parents in denial. But our foundation throughout has been the truth: In the face of all that has transpired, our story has never changed. We have not been intimidated, but have remained forthright and consistent in all our statements and efforts to uncover the facts surrounding our son's death in

Singapore. The same cannot be said of the Singapore police, IME, or even the U.S. State Department.

Christina and I have dedicated this book to our country. As average Americans, we are concerned for her future as we have witnessed first-hand how elected and public officials put personal ambition and power above truth and integrity. We know, as many of Shane's friends and colleagues know, and as the analysis of the suicide notes and the forensic evidence confirms, Shane did not commit suicide; rather he was the victim of a covert international power play, the extent of which still remains hidden.

In the beginning, we thought the SPF was merely incompetent: They never dusted for fingerprints, took DNA samples, secured the crime scene, checked for video surveillance, or conducted a real investigation. We now believe that it was not a case of incompetency, but that they were purposefully complicit in a cover up. In fact, it seems that their real incompetence was in how poorly they hid their deception. They tampered with photographic and digital evidence, provided conflicting stories about how Shane allegedly hanged himself, lied about how we acquired the hard drive and about taking pictures of Shane hanging from the bathroom door, and gave conflicting testimony on whether or not they used gloves to handle evidence.

The police additionally worked to suppress the testimony of Ashraf Massoud, the computer forensic expert, and delayed handing over evidence. Singapore's inquest was never a "non-adversarial fact finding mission." Singapore and IME hired ten top lawyers to prove the foregone conclusion of suicide. The coroner used a technical glitch to delay Dr. Adelstein's live video appearance, giving the police time to tamper with his testimony by sending him altered photographs of the body.

The coroner also permitted Shane's supervisor, Patrick Lo, to lie under oath about the relationship between Huawei and IME and Shane's training on the Veeco MOCVD machine. When our legal counsel presented an email proving Lo had given false information, the coroner refused to allow the document to be submitted as evidence, even though it was contained in the SPF's own evidentiary file.

Although the coroner berated Lo for attempting to coerce the testimony of six IME employees, he ultimately took no action against him. In fact, Romen Cubillo, who boldly defied Lo's intimidation tactics, was later fired from IME for his truthful statements. In October 2013, IME director Dr. Kwong requested a meeting with Romen. At this meeting, the representative from human resources stated, "Mr. Cubillo, you are under record, and since you said publically [at the inquest] that you are not happy with IME management, your contract is terminated today." Two security officers then gave Romen ten minutes to collect his things from his cubicle before escorting him out of the building. Romen has since reported this unjust firing to both the U.S. and French Embassies, but the issue of his being punished for his integrity in a court of law has never been addressed.

The coroner also delayed Rick's and my testimony beyond the date we were scheduled to leave Singapore, creating a hardship for us, but then refusing our request to have the testimony of the surprise witness, Luis Montes, postponed. This occurred in spite of the fact that Montes, who claims he was the last person to have seen Shane alive, was amenable to the postponement.

As we evaluated what transpired at the inquest, we also more fully realized the degree to which our legal team did not vigorously promote our case. Later it was revealed to us that our "pro bono" team had been compensated by the Chinese godmother of Gloria's husband and office manager, Gus, raising the question of whom they were actually serving.

Following the inquest, the coroner ruled that the evidence proves "beyond a reasonable doubt" that Shane committed suicide. This, in spite of all the facts to the contrary, that clearly raised more than considerable doubt. Then, for months, the coroner delayed releasing the inquest transcripts to us, even though he had used this official, verbatim record to issue his own findings.

Most recently, the coroner has again thwarted justice by ordering that the towel and strap that were allegedly found around Shane's neck be destroyed. As mentioned earlier, this towel and strap contained two prominent forms of DNA of Chinese and Malaysian origin. In an effort to preserve this important evidence, Rick and I hired a lawyer, Zhengxi Choo (Remy). Coroner Chay Yuen Fatt agreed to a disposal hearing on October 18, 2013, which Remy attended on our behalf.

At the hearing, State Counsel Tai Wei Shyong argued for the towel and strap's destruction and objected to its release for the following reasons:

(a) It was not normal for the implements of a suicide to be returned to the family of the suicide victim, ordinarily such implements would be disposed of;

(b) If the family wanted to forensically examine the implements, reasons would have to be given as to why;

(c) The implements of hanging were intimately bound up with the suicide and therefore should be disposed of; and

(d) The family has no proprietary entitlement to the implements of suicide.

Remy forcefully protested that the state counsel had not, prior to that morning's hearing, placed these objections in record. Thus, the family's counsel was unaware that the state would be taking a position and had not been given opportunity to prepare a rebuttal. Remy further argued that it was strange that the state had sent a legal representative to the hearing, considering that the question of whether the family wants to forensically examine the implements of hanging is not the state's business. Remy also noted that the family has a prima facie proprietary right to all the effects of the deceased, and, as a matter of law and principle, the family should not have to give reasons for obtaining such property.

Not surprisingly, the coroner sided with the state. He did order, however, that the implements of hanging be preserved for six months pending a formal request from the family in writing as to why they wanted them returned.

Rick and I retained Remy to appeal on our behalf and wrote a formal letter requesting that the items be returned to us.

On May 28, 2014, Remy relayed the following:

Dear Rick and Mary,

We regret to inform you that, despite our best efforts, the coroner today made the decision to have the towel and strap destroyed by the state.

We attach[ed] the set of rebuttal submissions we prepared which we believe clearly undermined the state's interpretation of the relevant statutes. Unfortunately, the coroner was not with us.

In so ruling, the coroner gave the following reasons:

1. The coroner had made a finding of suicide in the course of the inquiry;
2. Ordinarily, in suicides, the order would be for the police to destroy the property;
3. The family has not given reasons why the items should be returned;
4. The coroner did not want to cause the family further anguish by having the items remind them of the incident.

At the end of the disposal hearing, I asked for a stay of execution of the order for two weeks, during which time I would take your instructions on whether or not to have the Coroner's Order reviewed.

Should you decide to proceed with a judicial review in the High Court, I estimate the cost of the application to be in the region of S$10,000 in legal fees, not inclusive of about S$2,000 in filing fees and disbursements. We will have to take an amount of S$5,000 into account to begin work on this phase of proceedings.

I rate the chances of succeeding on review as an uphill task.

The reason for the amount involved in moving ahead is the length of time and the complexity of the issues implicated. When we came on board for you nearly a year ago, we did not expect the battle royale that would ensue on the issue of the return of the remaining items.

Call me if you have any questions.

Remy

As we had spent thousands of dollars and a great deal of effort trying to preserve the towel and the strap, we were outraged and insulted by Coroner Fatt's ruling and his reasoning that he "did not want to cause the family further anguish by having the items remind them of the incident." We decided, however, not to pursue the case any longer, as we knew further appeal would not change the outcome. Thus, to our knowledge, the state may have already incinerated the only known DNA evidence in Shane's case, without ever having it forensically examined against their DNA database.

Due to the opposition we faced from the police and state in Singapore, we desperately needed the resources and support of the U.S. government. Unfortunately, our government, specifically the State Department, has been more of a hindrance than a partner in seeking the truth. Nothing was more damaging to our case than the U.S. Embassy's rush to declare the Coroner's Inquiry and its findings "comprehensive, fair, and transparent." And as this occurred almost simultaneously with the report's release, it is doubtful anyone from the embassy even had the time to read the 145 page document before issuing that statement. Since then, the State Department has refused to retract this erroneous and unjust endorsement. They were also unwilling to step in to counteract the coroner's decision to destroy the DNA evidence found on the towel and strap.

The State Department has also obstructed the disclosure of truth by refusing to allow the written testimony of Vice Consul Traci Goins and U.S. Consul Craig Bryant. Traci was in the meeting when Detective Khal read the detailed description of how Shane supposedly hanged himself. She could refute Khal's testimony that he never read us that false description. Craig, who was involved in many meetings between the police and our lawyers, could likewise provide answers to important questions.

We always wanted to have Traci and Craig testify at the inquiry and we explicitly instructed our legal team to submit their names to the state counsel for inclusion as witnesses. In spite of our directive, however, our lawyers did not put their names on the witness list. Their explanation was, and remains, that Craig told them that he and Traci had diplomatic immunity and would not be able to testify. Craig also stated that to us directly. We have since been informed that this was not true. Various senior representatives at the U.S. Embassy, including Ambassador David Adelman, Deputy Chief Louis Mazel, and public affairs officer Eric Watnik, have stated that both Traci and Craig were "offered" to our counsel and the state counsel for testimony, in contradiction to the claims of both counsels. It is still unclear why we were deceived or who is responsible for this deception, but the result was the absence of critical testimony from Traci and Craig.

Despite written requests from Congressman Steve Daines, Congressman Frank Wolf, and Senator Max Baucus, the State Department has continued to deny us the written testimony of Tracy Goins and Craig Bryant. At one point, Senator Max Baucus told us that if we personally wrote a formal request, the State Department would comply. On February 12, 2014 we received the following response:

Dear Mr. and Mrs. Todd:

I write on behalf of the United States Department of State (the "Department") in response to your letter dated December 17, 2013. In your letter you requested written statements from Department employees Craig Bryant and Traci Goins regarding information acquired in the course and scope of the performance of their official duties for intended use in legal proceedings in Singapore.

The Department has reviewed your request in light of the factors set forth in 22 C.F.R. § 172.8, among other considerations, and respectfully declines to provide the statements you have requested. Accordingly, the Department has not authorized any employees to provide written statements or testimony in response to your request.

I regret that this may not be the answer you had hoped for. I again wish to express my condolences to you and your family for the loss of your son.

Sincerely,
Brett G. Pomainville, Chief
East Asia and Pacific Division
American Citizens Services and Crisis Management

The State Department's refusal to work on our behalf or even respond to our simple requests demonstrates how the Department has turned its back on the very citizens it is commissioned to serve, making any expression of condolence seem hollow and gratuitous. In our case, it appears that justice for an American family and legitimate national security concerns have been ignored either for political reasons or simply to placate international sensibilities. As a result of our treatment, I can't help but feel even greater sympathy for the family and friends of the four Americans murdered in Benghazi, Libya, who have experienced a similar State Department impasse in their pursuit of truth and justice.

The Justice Department and the FBI have been similarly unresponsive to our appeals for help. On April 18, 2013, prior to the Coroner's Inquiry, Senators Baucus and Tester wrote FBI Director, Robert Mueller, requesting that the FBI provide an independent pathology report and a forensic analysis of the alleged suicide notes for us to submit at the inquiry. A couple weeks later, Congressman Wolf wrote a letter to Robert Mueller, associating himself with this petition, and further emphasizing, "As you know from our conversations regarding this matter, I believe the FBI should thoroughly investigate this case both to help the Todd family learn the truth, as well as to understand any national security implications of the technology that may have been inappropriately transferred to Huawei or other foreign entities."

The FBI never complied with these appeals. They have also failed to respond to our requests for a meeting. On May 13, 2014, Congressman Daine's office sent us an email stating that the congressman had contacted the FBI to express frustration that the agency had been unresponsive to petitions for a meeting. Daine's office further stated, "We are told that the FBI will ask you to formally request a meeting with the appropriate FBI officials, such as the Deputy Assistant Director for International Relations, who is familiar with the case." The FBI has still not scheduled a meeting. The only call we received was from the FBI's victim protection agency, promising to take note of our requests.

In the meantime, Senator Baucus inexplicably ceased advocating for our case. On Friday, January 10, 2014, I received a call from Laura Rauch, Baucus' Military Legislative Assistant. It was not unusual for Laura to call, but this time she seemed colder and more formal. She began the conversation by listing all the ways Senator Baucus had helped our family. She then stated that, although the senator still cared deeply about our family and what happened to Shane, he no longer had the power to help us.

After thanking Laura for everything Baucus had done, I asked if, before he left office, the senator might put pressure on the embassy to give us Tracy Goins and Craig Bryant's written testimony and ask the FBI to meet with us. Laura responded that, as he was leaving office, Baucus would be unable to assist with this request. Later that afternoon, we discovered from a news report that Baucus had been appointed Ambassador to China by President Obama.

***

Our personal security and property have also been threatened. Our home was broken into on March 9, 2014, an incident which we reported to both the police and FBI. After that, we discovered that Shane's external Seagate hard drive and our hard copy of the Coroner's Inquest transcripts were missing. Fortunately, we have a copy of the hard drive in a secure location, and digital copies of the transcripts. We don't understand the motive for such theft, but it has made us realize that we are facing something much bigger and more sinister than we, as ordinary law-abiding citizens, could have ever imagined.

***

In the end, we may never discover why such forceful and concerted efforts were employed to make Shane's murder appear to be a suicide. It is highly doubtful that the individuals who personally orchestrated and carried out the murder will ever be discovered, tried, or punished. In that sense, justice may never be served in this life. But, ultimately, these individuals, whoever they are, are merely small players in a larger system of evil, corruption, and complicity which led to our son's murder and the corresponding cover-up. All those directly involved in the obstruction of truth, or who lacked the courage to stand up against it, are guilty too.

By telling Shane's story, we have obtained a certain degree of justice for him. In spite of all the effort exerted to suppress the truth, we have built a solid and convincing case. For our family, the case is closed; the verdict is homicide. It is now up to others, who value truth and justice, to take a stand and decide whether the same insidious powers that led to Shane's murder, and have no doubt destroyed the lives of many others, will be allowed to continue unabated.

In Memory of
Shane Truman Todd

(September 5, 1980–June 23, 2012)

The righteous perish, and no one ponders it in his heart; devout men are taken away, and no one understands that the righteous are taken way to be spared from evil. Those who walk uprightly enter into peace; they find rest as they lie in death.

Isaiah 57:1-2

Last Christmas Together,
December 25, 2011
(back row, left to right)
John and Shane;
(front row, left to right)
Chet, Corynne, Mary,
Rick, Dylan

Last Christmas Together,
December 2011
(left to right)
Shane, Chet, John, Dylan

Last Christmas Together,
December 2011
(left to right)
Dylan, Chet,
Corynne, Shane

*Shane and John
with their cousins,
Christina and Roston,
before the Kalispell Rodeo,
Summer 2002*

*Shane with his cousins,
Katie and Christina,
on the Fourth of July*

*Mary sending Shane off to
the Florida Science Fair*

Shane with Rick,
who is on a weekend break
from the U.S. Naval base
in Miramar, San Diego, California

Shane and John

Shane helping Chet
get ready for his wedding

Shane and Dylan

Shane with his brothers
in Whitefish, Montana:
(left to right)
Chet, Shane, Dylan, John

Shane at his
doctoral graduation from
University of California,
Santa Barbara

Shane reaching for the ball in a rugby game at
University of California, Santa Barbara

Shane kite-boarding
in Singapore

Shane and Shirley
in Singapore

EPILOGUE

In spite of our incredible loss and the difficult battle we have faced, our family is doing well. We are so proud of who Shane was and what he accomplished during his shortened life. He left a profound legacy.

In order to further his memory, Shane's grandmother, Jean Todd, has founded the Dr. Shane Truman Todd Memorial Science Center, in Pomona, California, where Shane spent his early childhood. People from all over are donating to make this center a reality. The center will honor Shane by providing a place for children to explore the wonderful world of science, so they might develop the same love for scientific inquiry and advancement that Shane possessed.

After Shane's death, Rick took a year off from flying. He has now returned to work, flying the Triple 7 for American Airlines. He has also established Truman Investments, along with our sons, in remembrance of Shane.

John, who is a pilot for Sky West, just got a job offer from American Airlines. Rick and John hope to have the opportunity to fly together, as captain and first officer, in the near future. John says that Shane's death has caused him to strive to be a better man and to live a life of which Shane would be proud.

On January 23, 2014, Chet and Corynne gave our family a gift beyond measure: our first grandson, who was named Truman, in honor of Shane. They have affectionately nicknamed him Tru. Tru has brought us incredible joy. Chet and Corynne are no longer running the family bed and breakfast. They bought and fixed up a charming Victorian home in Kalispell, Montana. Chet is selling real estate and continues to serve in the Air National Guard.

Dylan just graduated from the University of Montana with a degree in communications. After Shane's death, Dylan worked harder in school because he knew that would please Shane. Dylan says Shane's memory also inspires him to live as a man of integrity, like his oldest brother. Dylan is currently helping run Truman Investments and is representing one of the finest lines of handmade furniture in Montana.

Neither Rick nor I have been defeated by the sorrow, despair, or evil surrounding Shane's death. We believe that God has prepared us for such a time as this, and that with his help we have been capable of doing what he called us to do—pursue the truth in honor of Shane and for the sake of our country. We will miss our son every single day of our lives, but we are grateful for the rich blessings we've been given, and we constantly strive to become better, not bitter.

Writing this book, along with my niece, has been cathartic, and by God's grace "it is well with my soul."

—**Mary Todd**

Chet and Truman (Mary and Rick's grandson, who
was named in memory of Shane Truman Todd)

Acknowledgements

First and foremost, I want to thank my husband Rick, my best friend and indispensable partner. My niece and co-author, Christina Villegas, is like a daughter to me, and I could not have written this book without her skills and dedication. My brother and sister-in-law, Richard and Marty Elwell, have supported us immensely in our battle for truth and have expended great effort providing extensive and valuable feedback on the book. My sons, John, Chet, and Dylan, and my daughter-in-law, Corynne, have been a constant source of encouragement and joy in the midst of sorrow. Without Ray Bonner and Ashraf Massoud we wouldn't have a story to write. Ashraf engaged in hundreds of hours of computer forensic analysis, which gave Ray the ability to present Shane's story to the world. Jordan Doolittle designed the cover for the book and shanesharddrive.com, and Andy Kasinicky set up and maintains justice4shanetodd.com. We are also grateful to Carrie Lukas, Adriana Kazanjian, and others who helped edit or provided valuable feedback as we prepared our final manuscript. Last but not least, I want to thank our friends and family who have prayed for our strength, inspiration, and protection and have supported us in ways too numerous to recount.

About the Authors

Mary Todd has been married to Rick Todd for thirty-seven years. Together they are the proud parents of four sons, including Dr. Shane Truman Todd who was murdered in Singapore in June 2012.

Mary is an international speaker who earned her MA in Organizational Leadership from Azusa Pacific University, where she served as an assistant campus pastor. Currently, Mary is the pastor of a Pomona First Baptist satellite church in Marion, Montana. Since the morning she heard of her son's death, Mary has been a mother on a mission, intent on exposing evil and fighting for truth and justice. The Todd's story has been featured in the Financial Times, CNN, ABC, CBS, NBC, FOX News, several local and national newspapers and radio shows, an Asia One documentary, and 48 Hours.

Christina Villegas is Dr. Shane Truman Todd's cousin and one of his closest friends since childhood.

Christina holds a PhD in Politics from the Institute for Philosophic Studies at the University of Dallas, where she was an Earhart Fellow. She currently teaches American politics at California State University, San Bernardino and is a freelance writer. She has been interviewed on radio shows throughout the country and her research on public policy has been cited by a variety of media outlets including CNN, CSPAN, *The Atlantic,* the *New York Post,* and the *Huffington Post.*

Christina lives in Southern California with her husband Manuel.

Appendix A

THE ALLEGED SUICIDE NOTES

Dear Everyone,

I am very sorry it has come to this. I just want to make it clear that I do not blame anyone for my condition except myself. People at work have been patient and kind to me and have given me ample opportunity to succeed. My parents and family have given me more support than I could ask for. My friends in Singapore have been very kind and understanding and have tried to help me through this. And my girlfriend Shirley has been always loving and supportive even when it was no fun to hang out with me. She has been the most constant source of support, love, and friendship to me in Singapore and without her I wouldn't have made it this long.

I am so sorry it has come to this but I feel I am just a burden to those around me. I have tried to get jobs in the U.S. but I know I am not capable of fulfilling the duties required of me. I hope that you can remember the good things about me, about how I was loving son, grandson, brother, nephew, cousin, friend, boyfriend, co-worker and teammate. I had a few successes in life, so please try to remember my actions by those successes and not by the failure I have succumbed to.

I understand that this is a crime in Singapore. But for the sake of my family, I ask that you please be lenient and allow my family the ability to decide on what to do with me. If they wish to bring me back to the U.S., I ask you to please allow them to do so. I also ask that you allow them access to my bank account to pay for any expenses that arise. If you allow me to, I ask that my family decides what to do with any remaining money. I suggest giving the money to charity.

I am very sorry for the pain and trouble this causes. I never wanted to hurt anyone and I hope that you forgive me.

Love to all,

Shane Todd

Parents: Richard Todd and Mary Todd

Dear Mom and Dad,

I just want to let you know that I am so thankful for having you as my parents. You have given me the most love, patience, and support that any son could ask for. As you know I have been going through a difficult time and I am facing problems that I don't know how to solve. You both have given me such good advice but I don't have the strength or ability to follow through. I want to reiterate that none of this is your fault and despite the things I have said to you in the past, I am the only one to blame for my problems. I am so proud of the things you have built and the lives you have touched through your church and ministry. I hope that you understand that I am so sorry for the pain this causes. I just know how much of a burden I will be to you in the future so I feel it is better to do this now rather than wait until I have caused more damage.

You gave me so many great memories in life, spending time on the lake in Montana, going to the beach to drink Shirley Temples, bean dip at happy hour, fishing and snorkeling in the Keys, going to my countless sporting events, barbeques and family functions in our house on the hill, and going to church on Sundays. I hope that you cherish our good memories together. I love you very much.

Dear John, Chet, and Dylan,

I am so proud of the great men you guys have become. You guys are my best friends. I hope that you will always keep family close and have faith that God will bless your lives. I love you very much.

Dear Shirley,

You have been an angel to me. I know this will cause you great hurt but I know that you will be able to stay strong and rely on God to help you heal from this. You are so talented in so many ways and have a very bright future ahead of you. Please remember the good times we had and know that you are the best thing that happened to me while I was here in Singapore. I love you.

Dear Friends,

I thank you all for being a part of my life. Please remember the good times we had.

Again I am sorry and I hope you all forgive me.

Love,

Shane

Appendix B

Ashraf Massoud's Analysis of Shane's External Seagate Hard Drive

C209

DATACHASERS® INC

Forensic Computer Evidence Discovery, I.A.C.I.S. Certified
P.O. Box 2861, Riverside, CA 92516-2861 • www.DataChasers.com •
Admin@DataChasers.com
Direct: 951-780-7892 • Fax: 951-780-9199 • Nationwide: 877-DataExam [877-328-2392]
DataChasers® is a registered trademark of DataChasers, Incorporated   CDCA License PI-20551

CONFIDENTIAL MEMORANDUM

This communication is protected by confidentiality as intellectual property and/or the work product doctrine. Any and all content, information, or ideology, of any sort, contained herein are the confidential intellectual property of DataChasers® Inc., and are not to be shared or distributed, in any manner, outside the specific purpose of this engagement without the expressed written permission of an officer of the DataChasers® Corporation.

FROM: Ashraf Massoud, CFCE EnCE SCERS
             DATACHASERS® INC.

DATE: November 10, 2012

CASE: Shane Truman Todd

Subject: Forensic Analysis Findings

On July 24, 2012, I received the following external hard drive from Rick and Mary Todd, which they retrieved from Shane Todd's apartment;
     Seagate Free Agent Go S/N 2GE18WCK

Procedure:
The hard drive in question was imaged using Encase version 7.4.1.10. The hard drive was attached to the forensic laptop by way of a Tableau Write blocker. The image verified with no errors.

Objective:
Examine external drive to determine if drive had been accessed. Specifically, if the hard drive was accessed, when was it accessed and what files were accessed. To obtain a "big picture" of hard drive activity, the image was sorted and analyzed by the following dates:
- File Created -- date and time that a file was created on the drive
- Last Written -- date and time that a file written to, i.e. opened, viewed, and written to; in other words something was changed (added or deleted) within the contents of the file.
- Last Accessed -- date and time that a file was accessed, i.e. opened and viewed but not necessarily changed in content
- Entry Modified -- date and time that the Master File Table (MFT) information was changed

Facts:

Shane Todd was last seen alive on Friday, June 22, 2012, at 20:00 and found dead Sunday afternoon, June 24, 2012. Shane did not reply to phone calls or text messages from Friday evening on.

Assumptions:
Shane Todd was killed sometime between Friday evening and Sunday.

Analysis:

File Created
All files on the drive were sorted by the "File Created" date. In order to eliminate confusion of the timing of events, this study has adopted the use of a 24 hour clock. The analysis concentrated on all files created on June 22, 2012, and forward since Shane was known to be alive on the 22nd. The analysis of these dates revealed the following:

- The folder "C:\IME" and all of its contents, a total of 3,132 files, were created between 11:39:06 and 11:42:18
- 3 files created at 15:25:21 in the folder "C:\" System Information"
- 1 file created at 17:09:41 in the folder "C:\IME\My Documents\Research\NEMS Switch"

This was done in an attempt to create a baseline of activity on the hard drive during a time Shane was known to be alive. Considering this activity, it would appear that Shane performed a "back up" of the files located in C:\IME. Since these files were being created within seconds of each other, it would suggest that he "dragged and dropped" this folder from the computer hard drive onto this external hard drive for back up purposes. Later, around 15:25, the computer that the hard drive was attached to performed what appears to be a Restore Point. This action would be the result of an automatic function of the computer that this external hard drive was attached to not human input. At approximately 17:09 the last file to be created on this hard drive was called 2012-06-21 IEDM Togglefin.docx in the C:\IME\MyDocuments\Research\NEMS Switch folder. No other files were created on this hard drive for the remainder of 6/22/12.

Last Written
Files were then sorted by the "Last Written" date and the last file that was written to on 6/22/12 was at 16:14:30 at the following location:
C:\System Volume Information_restore{1AABEF77-E9F4-4F47-85E2-760AE63BEFBF}\RP406\RestorePointSize.
No other files were "written" to for the remainder of 6/22/12.

However, of interest is the fact that on Saturday 6/23/12 between 03:40:50 and 03:42:23 the following folders were written too, meaning they were opened and viewed for whatever reason, but the contents of the folders were not changed:

- C\IME\My Documents\Research\NEMS Switch\Process Development
- C\IME\My Documents\Research\NEMS Switch\Project Plans\Electrostatic
- C\IME\My Documents\Research\NEMS Switch\IEDM
- C\IME\My Documents\Research\NEMS Switch\Summary
- C\IME\My Documents\Research\NEMS Switch
- C\System Volume Information\EfaData

Then at 17:47:13 on 6/23/12 the following files were Last Written to:

- C\System Volume Information\EfaData\sdmys_AB6CC62562B292B1A38FBD26
- C\System Volume Information\EfaData\sdmys_AB6CC62562B292B125E0EA64
- C\System Volume Information\EfaData\SYMEFA.DB

Based on research, the above three files (highlighted in green) are most likely associated with a Norton product.

Of even greater significance, is the fact that no other access occurred on this hard drive throughout the remainder of 6/23/12 through 6/27/12, until the following folders and file were accessed on June 27, 2012, between 20:38:39 and 20:40:28, three (3) days AFTER Shane's body was discovered and removed from his apartment.

The following are the folders accessed after Shane's death:

- C\My Documents 2010-11-27\Miscellaneous
- C\IME\My Documents\Goal Setting
- C\IME\My Documents\IME\Supervisor
- C\IME\My Documents
- C\IME\My Documents\~$characterization result to veeco.pptx

Again the contents of the folders where not changed, but the folders were opened (causing them to be written to) to see what was in them. The last item listed above was actually deleted on 6/27/12.

Last Accessed
Since writing to a file requires access to that file, the same files that were written to under the "Last Written" analysis were also "Last Accessed" on the same date and time and therefore a repeat of the same analysis is not necessary here.

It is important to ask who accessed this hard drive in the early morning and late afternoon of 6/23/12, and again on 6/27/12. Shane was likely dead on 6/23, and definitely dead on the 6/24. This is highly suspicious as the hard drive does not have its own operating system and needs a computer hooked up to it in order to record this data. If the police took Shane's computer as reported, then the question needs to be asked, "what is this external hard drive attached to?"

Entry Modified
Entry Modified, refers to when the Master File Table (MFT) entry for that file was last changed. The MFT entry contains a lot of information about the file, including size, name, location on the disk, parent folder, creation date, etc. Changing any one of these should also change the "Entry Modified" date, i.e. renaming the file, accessing the file, writing to the file, moving the file (defragmenting – moving it on the disk, or moving it into a different folder), or increasing the file size. Under normal circumstances, any action that trips any of the other dates, created, accessed, or last written, will also trip the Entry Modified date. This is due to one of two reasons:
- The action that tripped the date, e.g. renaming the file caused a change in the MFT so the Entry Modified date will be updated.
- Altering any of the file dates will, by definition, change the MFT Entry (as this is where the dates are stored). Therefore the MFT Entry is changed.

In the present case, the MFT records show a change for the following files on 6/27/12 20:36:59 and 20:40:28:

- C\System Volume Information\MountPointManagerRemoteDatabase
- C\My Documents 2010-11-27\Miscellaneous\sheriff_letter.doc
- C\My Documents 2010-11-27\Miscellaneous
- C\IME\My Documents\Goal Setting\2011-07-12 _ Goal Setting Shane.xlsx
- C\IME\My Documents\Goal Setting
- C\IME\My Documents\IME\Supervisor\Shane Todd _ AGS Supervisor.docx
- C\IME\My Documents\IME\Supervisor
- C\IME\My Documents\characterization result to veeco.pptx
- C\IME\My Documents\~$characterization result to veeco.pptx
- C\IME\My Documents

To restate, the MFT entry changes whenever something regarding a file or folder changes. Since certain files and folders were accessed on 6/27/12, their respective MFT entries also changed. In the list above, there are a couple of files that were not mentioned in the previous "last accessed or last written" section and yet their MFT entry records shows 6/27/12. It is unclear why their MFT entry were changed, perhaps the properties of the files were checked and therefore only their MFT record would change.

Conclusion:

The significant components of this report to consider are: who had access to Shane's external hard drive, what was accessed, and when were they accessed? The forensic analysis supports that the external hard drive activity occurred three (3) days after Shane's death and three (3) days after local police seized his computer.

This access occurred within 24 hours of when Shane's family arrived at the apartment to collect his personal affects. How were these files either accessed, written to, or the MFT modified after Shane's death? It is also important to note, that these files that had been accessed and/or written to, are not just system (non-user files), they were very specific folders and user files which required human intervention and not the result of an auto scanning program.

The findings in this forensic analysis report cannot be 100% conclusive without Shane's actual computers. They are necessary in order to determine if it was one or both of his computers that was connected to his back up hard drive or, instead, an entirely different computer that was connected to it. Until then, this forensic investigation is ongoing.

Should you have any questions or concerns, you are welcome to call me.

Sincerely,

[signature]

Ashraf Massoud, EnCE, CFCE, SCERS
909.266.6825

CPSIA information can be obtained at www.ICGtesting.com
Printed in the USA
LVOW11s0756230714

395549LV00001B/1/P